No Lex 10-12

PEACHTREE CITY
PLAN TO STAY™

PEACHTREE CITY LIBRARY
201 Willowbend Road
Peachtree City, GA 30269-1623
Phone: 770-631-2520
Fax: 770-631-2522

CHARLIE PARKER

CHARLIE PARKER

Ron Frankl

Senior Consulting Editor
Nathan Irvin Huggins
Director
W.E.B. Du Bois Institute for Afro-American Research
Harvard University

CHELSEA HOUSE PUBLISHERS
Philadelphia

Chelsea House Publishers
Editor-in-Chief Richard S. Papale
Managing Editor Karyn Gullen Browne
Copy Chief Philip Koslow
Picture Editor Adrian G. Allen
Art Director Nora Wertz
Manufacturing Director Gerald Levine
Systems Manager Lindsey Ottman
Production Coordinator Marie Claire Cebrián-Ume

Black Americans of Achievement
Senior Editor Richard Rennert

Staff for CHARLIE PARKER
Copy Editor Margaret Dornfeld
Editorial Assistant Nicole Greenblatt
Designer Diana Blume
Picture Researcher Pat Burns
Cover Illustration Daniel Mark Duffy

5 7 9 8 6

Library of Congress Cataloging-in-Publication Data
Frankl, Ron.
   Charlie Parker, musician/by Ron Frankl
   p. cm.—(Black Americans of achievement)
   Includes bibliographical references and index.
  Summary: Introduces the life and times of the noted jazz musician
Charlie Parker.
  ISBN   0-7910-1134-8
        0-7910-1159-3 (pbk.)
   1. Parker, Charlie, 1920–1955—Juvenile literature. 2. Jazz
musicians—United States—Biography—Juvenile literature. 3.
Afro-American musicians—Biography—Juvenile literature. [1. Parker,
Charlie, 1920–1955. 2. Musicians. 3. Afro-Americans—Biography.
4. Jazz.] I. Title. II. Series.
ML3930.P24F7 1992
788.7'3165'092—dc20
[B]
                                                  92-12126
                                                       CIP
                                                   AC MN

Frontispiece: *Known as Bird to his
friends and adoring fans, saxophonist
Charlie Parker performs in 1947
with bassist Tommy Potter (left) and
trumpeter Miles Davis (right) at the
Three Deuces in New York City.*

CONTENTS

On Achievement   8
Coretta Scott King

1
"Parker's Mood"   11

2
"K.C. Blues"   21

3
"Carvin' the Bird"   29

4
"Cool Blues"   39

5
"Hootie Blues"   47

6
"Ornithology"   59

7
"Now's the Time"   67

8
"Chasin' the Bird"   77

9
"Relaxin' at Camarillo"   89

10
"Celebrity"   99

11
"Bird of Paradise"   111

Appendix: Selected Discography   121

Chronology   122

Further Reading   124

Index   125

BLACK AMERICANS OF ACHIEVEMENT

HENRY AARON
baseball great

KAREEM ABDUL-JABBAR
basketball great

RALPH ABERNATHY
civil rights leader

ALVIN AILEY
choreographer

MUHAMMAD ALI
heavyweight champion

RICHARD ALLEN
*religious leader and
social activist*

MAYA ANGELOU
author

LOUIS ARMSTRONG
musician

ARTHUR ASHE
tennis great

JOSEPHINE BAKER
entertainer

JAMES BALDWIN
author

BENJAMIN BANNEKER
scientist and mathematician

AMIRI BARAKA
poet and playwright

COUNT BASIE
bandleader and composer

ROMARE BEARDEN
artist

JAMES BECKWOURTH
frontiersman

MARY McLEOD BETHUNE
educator

JULIAN BOND
civil rights leader and politician

GWENDOLYN BROOKS
poet

JIM BROWN
football great

BLANCHE BRUCE
politician

RALPH BUNCHE
diplomat

STOKELY CARMICHAEL
civil rights leader

GEORGE WASHINGTON
CARVER
botanist

RAY CHARLES
musician

CHARLES CHESNUTT
author

JOHN COLTRANE
musician

BILL COSBY
entertainer

PAUL CUFFE
merchant and abolitionist

COUNTEE CULLEN
poet

ANGELA DAVIS
civil rights leader

BENJAMIN DAVIS, SR., AND
BENJAMIN DAVIS, JR.
military leaders

SAMMY DAVIS, JR.
entertainer

FATHER DIVINE
religious leader

FREDERICK DOUGLASS
abolitionist editor

CHARLES DREW
physician

W. E. B. DU BOIS
scholar and activist

PAUL LAURENCE DUNBAR
poet

KATHERINE DUNHAM
dancer and choreographer

DUKE ELLINGTON
bandleader and composer

RALPH ELLISON
author

JULIUS ERVING
basketball great

JAMES FARMER
civil rights leader

ELLA FITZGERALD
singer

MARCUS GARVEY
black nationalist leader

JOSH GIBSON
baseball great

DIZZY GILLESPIE
musician

PRINCE HALL
social reformer

W. C. HANDY
father of the blues

WILLIAM HASTIE
educator and politician

MATTHEW HENSON
explorer

CHESTER HIMES
author

BILLIE HOLIDAY
singer

JOHN HOPE
educator

LENA HORNE
entertainer

LANGSTON HUGHES
poet

ZORA NEALE HURSTON
author

JESSE JACKSON
civil rights leader and politician

MICHAEL JACKSON
entertainer

JACK JOHNSON
heavyweight champion

JAMES WELDON JOHNSON
author

SCOTT JOPLIN
composer

BARBARA JORDAN
politician

CORETTA SCOTT KING
civil rights leader

MARTIN LUTHER KING, JR.
civil rights leader

SPIKE LEE
filmmaker

REGINALD LEWIS
entrepreneur

ALAIN LOCKE
scholar and educator

JOE LOUIS
heavyweight champion

RONALD MCNAIR
astronaut

MALCOLM X
militant black leader

THURGOOD MARSHALL
Supreme Court justice

TONI MORRISON
author

CONSTANCE BAKER MOTLEY
civil rights leader and judge

ELIJAH MUHAMMAD
religious leader

EDDIE MURPHY
entertainer

JESSE OWENS
champion athlete

SATCHEL PAIGE
baseball great

CHARLIE PARKER
musician

GORDON PARKS
photographer

ROSA PARKS
civil rights leader

SIDNEY POITIER
actor

ADAM CLAYTON POWELL, JR.
political leader

COLIN POWELL
military leader

LEONTYNE PRICE
opera singer

A. PHILIP RANDOLPH
labor leader

PAUL ROBESON
singer and actor

JACKIE ROBINSON
baseball great

DIANA ROSS
entertainer

BILL RUSSELL
basketball great

JOHN RUSSWURM
publisher

SOJOURNER TRUTH
antislavery activist

HARRIET TUBMAN
antislavery activist

NAT TURNER
slave revolt leader

DENMARK VESEY
slave revolt leader

ALICE WALKER
author

MADAM C. J. WALKER
entrepreneur

BOOKER T. WASHINGTON
educator and racial spokesman

IDA WELLS-BARNETT
civil rights leader

WALTER WHITE
civil rights leader

OPRAH WINFREY
entertainer

STEVIE WONDER
musician

RICHARD WRIGHT
author

ON ACHIEVEMENT

Coretta Scott King

BEFORE YOU BEGIN this book, I hope you will ask yourself what the word *excellence* means to you. I think that it's a question we should all ask, and keep asking as we grow older and change. Because the truest answer to it should never change. When you think of excellence, perhaps you think of success at work; or of becoming wealthy; or meeting the right person, getting married, and having a good family life.

Those important goals are worth striving for, but there is a better way to look at excellence. As Martin Luther King, Jr., said in one of his last sermons, "I want you to be first in love. I want you to be first in moral excellence. I want you to be first in generosity. If you want to be important, wonderful. If you want to be great, wonderful. But recognize that he who is greatest among you shall be your servant."

My husband, Martin Luther King, Jr., knew that the true meaning of achievement is service. When I met him, in 1952, he was already ordained as a Baptist preacher and was working toward a doctoral degree at Boston University. I was studying at the New England Conservatory and dreamed of accomplishments in music. We married a year later, and after I graduated the following year we moved to Montgomery, Alabama. We didn't know it then, but our notions of achievement were about to undergo a dramatic change.

You may have read or heard about what happened next. What began with the boycott of a local bus line grew into a national movement, and by the time he was assassinated in 1968 my husband had fashioned a black movement powerful enough to shatter forever the practice of racial segregation. What you may not have read about is where he got his method for resisting injustice without compromising his religious beliefs.

He adopted the strategy of nonviolence from a man of a different race, who lived in a different country, and even practiced a different religion. The man was Mahatma Gandhi, the great leader of India, who devoted his life to serving humanity in the spirit of love and nonviolence. It was in these principles that Martin discovered his method for social reform. More than anything else, those two principles were the key to his achievements.

This book is about black Americans who served society through the excellence of their achievements. It forms a part of the rich history of black men and women in America—a history of stunning accomplishments in every field of human endeavor, from literature and art to science, industry, education, diplomacy, athletics, jurisprudence, even polar exploration.

Not all of the people in this history had the same ideals, but I think you will find something that all of them had in common. Like Martin Luther King, Jr., they all decided to become "drum majors" and serve humanity. In that principle—whether it was expressed in books, inventions, or song—they found something outside themselves to use as a goal and a guide. Something that showed them a way to serve others, instead of only living for themselves.

Reading the stories of these courageous men and women not only helps us discover the principles that we will use to guide our own lives but also teaches us about our black heritage and about America itself. It is crucial for us to know the heroes and heroines of our history and to realize that the price we paid in our struggle for equality in America was dear. But we must also understand that we have gotten as far as we have partly because America's democratic system and ideals made it possible.

We are still struggling with racism and prejudice. But the great men and women in this series are a tribute to the spirit of our democratic ideals and the system in which they have flourished. And that makes their stories special and worth knowing. ❦

1

"PARKER'S MOOD"

IT WAS SUPPOSED to be his big comeback, his return to the spotlight after several years of personal and professional problems that had practically ended his career as a jazz musician. As 34-year-old Charlie Parker waited to take the stage on March 4, a Friday night in 1955, he knew that his next several performances could begin a new era in his life, one in which he might reclaim the success he had won only a few years earlier. He also realized that his weekend engagement at Birdland, New York City's foremost jazz club, might be his last chance.

Birdland, billed as the Jazz Corner of the World, stood on Broadway near 52nd Street, in a small patch of midtown that was *the* place to hear jazz. Back in 1949, when the club first opened its doors to the public, Parker was extended the honor of having the night spot named after him. It had seemed logical to call Birdland after Parker, whose nickname of Yardbird was often shortened to Bird by his adoring friends and fans. After all, he was the greatest young talent in jazz.

Just a few years prior to the opening of Birdland, when Parker was still in his mid-twenties, the alto saxophonist had forever changed the direction of jazz with his revolutionary approach to harmony and rhythm. This new style, called bebop (or simply bop), departed from the dance-oriented "swing" style of jazz

"Music is your own experience, your thoughts, your wisdom," Charlie Parker observed. "If you don't live it, it won't come out of your horn."

11

that had been popular for a decade. Bebop stressed improvisation over conventional melody and featured unusual harmonies and rhythmic shifts. It demanded the full attention of the listener and was anything but background music. At its best, bebop was daring, thrilling music that was both intellectually and emotionally challenging. And when he was healthy and happy, nobody played bebop better than Charlie Parker.

Parker's music was the perfect balance of creativity, virtuosity, spontaneity, and emotion. Although his sound was often imitated, it was seldom surpassed. Every young jazz musician who heard Parker's music was in some way influenced by his ideas. Even some of the older, more traditional-minded musicians were inspired and revitalized by his stunning innovations.

Parker was not bebop's only pioneer. A handful of other young musicians, most notably trumpeters Miles Davis and John ("Dizzy") Gillespie and pianists Thelonious Monk and Bud Powell, helped usher in the new sound. But Parker was regarded as the most talented musician of the bebop revolution; and even though he was far better known among jazz musicians and serious fans than with the general public, he seemed to have the brightest of futures.

Parker's popularity increased slowly through 1948, and by the following year his records were selling well for the first time in his career. He and his quintet also reached thousands of listeners through their exciting early morning performances broadcast weekly on the radio from the Royal Roost nightclub. The public, it seemed, was finally beginning to appreciate the musical genius of Charlie Parker.

Parker was enjoying his growing fame. In May 1949, he made a triumphant concert tour of Europe, where he was greeted by wildly enthusiastic audiences everywhere he performed. Six months later, he realized a long-standing dream by recording with a string

orchestra. Among bebop musicians, only friend and former bandmate Dizzy Gillespie surpassed Bird in popularity as 1949 drew to a close.

On December 15, 1949, Birdland's opening night, Parker had stood at the pinnacle of his popularity. A large crowd jammed the club to hear an all-star roster of jazz performers. Included in the show were saxophonist Lester Young, Parker's idol when he was a teenager; another brilliant saxophonist, Stan Getz; and an exciting new singer named Harry Belafonte. Headlining the bill was Parker himself.

Yet only five years later, on a Saturday night in March, Parker was desperately trying to reestablish himself in a jazz scene he had helped create. Many of his former associates had become major concert, nightclub, and recording stars, playing music that was often only a weaker version of his own ideas. Musicians were growing rich from the style and vision

Heading a group of jazz all-stars, Parker opens Birdland, the New York City nightclub named after him, on December 15, 1949. Accompanying the 29-year-old saxophonist on this gala occasion were (from left to right) trumpeter Max Kaminsky, saxophonist Lester Young, trumpeter Oran Page, and pianist Lennie Tristano.

of Charlie Parker, yet he was homeless and often had to stay with friends for days or weeks at a time. On several occasions, he even slept on park benches and subway trains.

By March 1955, Parker was a forgotten man to many in the music world. It was a tragic situation, made sadder still by the fact that he was largely to blame for his own troubles. Years of erratic behavior, worsened by heroin and alcohol abuse, had severely damaged his reputation in the music industry, and it had become difficult for him to find opportunities to perform.

Parker's heroin use had also gotten him in trouble with the New York City Police Department. As a result, in 1951 he had lost his cabaret card, a permit issued by the New York State Liquor Authority to all performers who wished to work in New York City nightclubs. Even though Parker was not convicted of drug possession or any other crime, the police recommended that his cabaret card be suspended. Without it, he could not work in any of the city's night spots.

By the time Parker was finally issued another cabaret card in 1953, his reputation and career had been ruined. He had landed the March 1955 gig at Birdland only by pleading with his booking agent, who had finally agreed to arrange the saxophonist's return to the stage. This show would mark Parker's first appearance at the nightclub since a troubled engagement the previous summer, during which he had fired the accompanying string orchestra in mid-performance! For that unprofessional outburst, he had been barred from performing at Birdland.

Parker's personal life was also very troubled. He and Chan Parker, his common-law wife, had split up at the end of 1954, and he seemed entirely lost without her. His years with Chan had provided him with the only period of domestic happiness and stability he had experienced since childhood; she had seemed to understand him better than any of the other women in his life. Without her, he seemed to lose the will to fight the troubles that now all but overwhelmed him.

As if all these problems were not bad enough, Parker's health was also beginning to fail. He was once the hardiest of men, but years of overindulgence in heroin, alcohol, and food had taken their toll. He had suffered from heart trouble for years, and even though he had finally managed to kick his heroin habit, the liquor he used as a substitute worsened his severe stomach ulcers.

Parker knew that his comeback weekend at Birdland was an opportunity to regain control of his life, to dig in and fight back, to reclaim the commercial and artistic success that should have been his. Aware of this, Birdland's management had assembled a band consisting of musicians who had shared some of Parker's earlier triumphs.

On trumpet was McKinley ("Kenny") Dorham, who had played in Parker's group six years earlier. Drummer Art Blakey and bassist Charles Mingus had performed intermittently with Parker for several years and would soon be leading their own groundbreaking bands. Rounding out the quintet was Bud Powell, whose style on the piano was almost as innovative as Parker's on the saxophone.

Sadly, Powell had been suffering from mental disorders for many years. His behavior was even less predictable than Parker's, and his career had suffered greatly as a result. When Powell was in good mental health, he was a more than worthy accompanist for Parker. But when he was experiencing a mental disturbance or was drinking, Powell was completely undependable and quite uncontrollable.

The Friday-night shows went fairly well, although Powell's behavior was typically erratic. At one point in the evening, he insulted Parker without provoca-

The mood at Birdland for Parker's comeback engagement on March 5, 1955, was much different from that of the club's opening night, as a wary Art Blakey, seated behind his drum kit (right), eyes an extremely gifted but mentally unstable Bud Powell. Moments later, the pianist drew Parker into a quarrel onstage, causing the performance to end suddenly, on a bitterly disappointing note.

tion while the saxophonist spoke quietly with pianist Lennie Tristano between sets. Parker, though, did not seem particularly upset by Powell's actions on the first evening of the two-night engagement.

Saturday night proved a much different story. Birdland was crowded, and Bird was late for the first set. The four other musicians decided to go onstage and entertain the audience until he arrived. Powell was drunk and angry, however, and the music that

emerged from the bandstand was harsh and disorganized. Blakey, Dorham, and Mingus were among the most professional of musicians and did their best to cover for the disturbed pianist. Yet Powell, Dorham recalled, "was in no fit mental condition" to perform.

Parker arrived half an hour into the set. He exchanged several angry words with Oscar Goodstein, the manager of the nightclub, who chided the musician for his tardiness. After that, Parker decided to sit out the rest of the first set. Already the evening was off to a bad start.

Parker retired to the dressing room and poured himself a drink to relax. When the other musicians stopped in after the set, he talked quietly with Blakey. By the time the second show drew near, Parker appeared eager to perform. Apparently he was unaware of Powell's deteriorating condition.

One by one the musicians filed onstage, where Parker introduced his fellow performers to an enthusiastic audience. Then he called out the first tune, an original composition entitled "Hallucinations." As Parker, Blakey, Dorham, and Mingus began the song, Powell launched into "Little Willie Leaps." Parker immediately stopped the music and patiently repeated his instructions. He counted off the tempo for the tune once again, but Powell still played the other song.

Now Parker grew angry. "Come on, baby!" he urged the pianist.

Powell turned to face his leader, grinned drunkenly, and swore at him. Parker growled back, and the two men continued to curse at each other before a shocked audience. The other musicians could only watch in horror.

Finally, Powell slammed his elbow against the keyboard, stood up, and left the stage. Parker turned quickly toward the audience and said, "Ladies and gentlemen, I'm sorry to say our most brilliant member has deserted us."

But instead of trying to salvage the evening by carrying on without Powell, Parker tried to induce the pianist to come back to the stage. "Bud Powell! Bud Powell!" Parker shouted into the microphone, speaking the man's name each time in a more mechanical and monotonous voice.

Powell did not return. And yet Parker continued to shout over and over into the microphone, his voice filling the nightclub. The other musicians fumbled with their instruments or looked away in embarrassment as Parker went on and on, calling "Bud Powell!" throughout the otherwise quiet room. The customers began to get up from their tables and leave the nightclub. There would be no more music. The show was over.

Dejected, Charlie Parker stood alone on the bandstand for several minutes as the crowd exited. Finally, he too left Birdland. ❧

2

"K.C. BLUES"

CHARLIE PARKER'S LIFE began far away from New York City, the scene of his greatest triumphs and tragedies. He spent his early years in and around Kansas City, Missouri, a wild and rough boomtown that served as a business and entertainment center for much of the western United States during the first half of the 20th century. Kansas City was, then as now, a cattle town, where vast numbers of the animals were bought, sold, slaughtered, butchered, and finally sent to all corners of the nation.

Kansas City was also well known for its political corruption. Dedicated only to making money and retaining power, the city's government officials bought votes and influence in exchange for political favors. Because local government and organized crime were virtually one in these politicians' hands, the city developed a well-earned reputation for allowing all kinds of vice, including gambling and prostitution.

The height of lawlessness occurred between 1919 and 1933, the years when the manufacture and sale of alcohol was illegal in the United States. Prohibition went virtually unnoticed in Kansas City. Saloons and nightclubs flourished throughout the city, and the music of choice in these establishments was jazz.

Parker at age two. The future jazz giant was born in Kansas City, Kansas, a suburb of the much larger Missouri city along the eastern bank of the Kaw River.

21

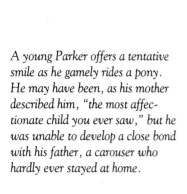

A young Parker offers a tentative smile as he gamely rides a pony. He may have been, as his mother described him, "the most affectionate child you ever saw," but he was unable to develop a close bond with his father, a carouser who hardly ever stayed at home.

The first music to be called jazz evolved in New Orleans, Louisiana, around 1900. A mixture of blues, ragtime, spirituals, folk, and brass-band music, jazz rapidly gained popularity throughout the country. By 1920, it had spread from New Orleans to such faraway cities as Chicago, New York, and Washington, D.C. Kansas City, with its wide-open entertainment scene, soon emerged as a hotbed for jazz. It also became a magnet for jazz musicians, who were attracted by the large number of job opportunities in the city's many night spots. If only a few musicians managed to grow rich in Kansas City, an even smaller amount failed to find work there.

Charlie Parker's birth coincided with the rise of Kansas City jazz. He was born Charles Parker, Jr., on August 29, 1920, in Kansas City, Kansas. The town of his birth was a suburb of the much larger Kansas City just across the Kaw River in Missouri. The entire metropolitan area, which included both Kansas Cities, boasted about 500,000 residents in 1920. Approximately 15 percent of the population was black.

Charlie's father, who hailed from Memphis, Tennessee, made his living as a singer and dancer on the black vaudeville circuit. At the end of one of these black theater tours, he found himself stranded in Kansas City. There he met 17-year-old Addie Boyley, a Kansas City native who soon became his wife and Charlie's mother. Charlie had a half brother, John, who was his father's child from a relationship with another woman. John did not live with the Parkers, so the future jazz giant was essentially an only child. He was also, according to his mother, "the most affectionate child you ever saw. When he was two he'd come to the door and say, 'Mama, you there?' And I'd say, 'Yes, I'm here,' and he'd go on playing. Since he could talk he'd say, 'Mama, I love you.'"

Charlie's relationship with his father was not quite so affectionate. Charles Parker, Sr., never lost his taste for life on the road, not even after his days as a professional entertainer had come to a close. Shortly after Charlie's birth, the former vaudeville entertainer took a job as a chef for a railroad company, which kept him away from Kansas City for long stretches at a time.

Charles, Sr., tried to be a good husband and father, but apparently it was not in his nature. After a while, he began to disappear from home for even lengthier periods and to see other women. Alcoholism was part of the problem.

On those rare occasions when Charles, Sr., was at home, he liked to play the piano and sing, even though his talents were somewhat limited. These impromptu performances served as Charlie's earliest exposure to music. The youngster also grew up listening to his father's phonograph, which was something of a luxury item for black families in the mid-1920s. Charles, Sr., possessed a collection of the most recent jazz and blues recordings, which allowed his young son to become acquainted with the music of trumpeter Louis Armstrong, pianist Duke Ellington, vocalist Bessie Smith, and others.

When Charlie was about eight years old, he moved with his parents from sleepy Kansas City, Kansas, to the larger Missouri city across the river. They rented a house at 1516 Olive Street in the heart of Kansas City's black district, which covered an area of six square blocks. The house stood within walking distance of most of the city's nightclubs and saloons, and it remained Charlie's home until he was an adult.

Shortly after Charlie and his parents settled into their Olive Street home, his father left the family for good. "He could dance; he was a good scholar; he could play the piano," Addie Parker said of her husband, "but he was a drunkard. I tried so many times to get him to stop but all he would say was, 'Ten years from today I will stop drinking.'" He never did. Eight years after he abandoned his wife and son, Charles Parker, Sr., was killed during a drunken quarrel.

With only his mother to rely on, Charlie reinforced his close bond with Addie Parker. A remarkably strong and capable woman who worked hard to provide the best possible life for her son, she supported him by cleaning the homes of white families.

Although Addie usually worked long hours, she would not allow Charlie to take a part-time job to help her out. Her fondest dream was that he would

Parker's mother, Addie, encouraged her only child to excel in the classroom throughout his boyhood, and he responded with flying colors until he took up the saxophone in his first year at Lincoln High School. He immediately became so enamored with the musical instrument that he neglected his studies and put all his energy into improving his playing skills.

become a doctor, and she wanted him to have all the time he needed to concentrate on his schoolwork, even if it meant she had to toil late into the night to make ends meet. There was every reason to believe her wish would come true. Charlie was an especially bright child and received good grades at Attucks Public School. He was well liked by his teachers; one of them even told his mother, "Your boy is going to amount to something."

It was clear that that "something" would not be in the field of athletics, for Charlie never showed the slightest interest in sports. His favorite hobby was reading. He also liked music, although he did not have the slightest idea how to play an instrument. That would soon change.

After Charlie turned 13 years old, he entered Lincoln High, a large, racially segregated public school that was extremely overcrowded. The institution's meager financial resources only helped to lower its already substandard quality of education. Unhappy with the conditions at his new school, Charlie grew bored with his studies.

Fortunately for Charlie, Lincoln High boasted an outstanding music department. Its marching and concert bands had long been prominent attractions in Kansas City parades and ceremonies, with many of the band members going on to pursue musical careers. Charlie decided to take advantage of the school's sole strength. During his freshman year, he enrolled in a music course and was assigned to the baritone horn. He found the instrument relatively easy to master, in part because, in the band's musical arrangements, the baritone horn was usually limited to a simple pattern of low notes.

Charlie quickly became disenchanted with the large brass instrument. He preferred the saxophone, which produced a far more melodic sound, the kind he heard emanating from the clubs he passed on his way to and from school. Charlie thought the alto saxophone had to be the most glamorous instrument of all, and he persuaded his mother to buy him one.

Addie Parker could not afford a new saxophone, so she purchased an old one for $45 (which was several weeks' wages). The instrument Charlie received was more than 30 years old and in poor condition; it had to be repaired before he could use it. Even then, the decrepit saxophone did not produce much of a sound.

Undeterred, Charlie decided to make learning how to play the saxophone the most important activity in his life. The interest he had previously shown in schoolwork was directed toward his new hobby. Before long, he felt confident enough in his playing to join a few of his friends from Lincoln High in a band called the Deans of Swing. Charlie was the youngest member of the group, which performed mostly at dances and parties. He was also its least skilled musician.

"It was the first band Bird ever worked in, and he seemed to me then just like a happy-go-lucky kid," recalled bassist Gene Ramey, a member of the Deans of Swing who went on to enjoy a successful career as a musician. "Bird wasn't doing anything, musically speaking, at that period. In fact, he was the saddest thing in the band, and the other members gave him something of a hard time."

It would be several years before Charlie's enthusiasm for music would be matched by his skill. Still, he refused to become discouraged. He kept on practicing on his beat-up old alto, and slowly he became a competent saxophonist. By the age of 14, he was convinced that his future lay in music.

The unfortunate result of Charlie's wholehearted commitment to music was that it virtually ended his formal education. He had neglected his studies so completely after taking up the saxophone that when he returned to Lincoln High School to begin his sophomore year, he was told he was being left back. Rather than reorder his priorities and salvage his education, Charlie decided to skip school most of the time and concentrate on improving his musical skills. This decision would determine the course of the rest of his life. Charlie Parker was, now and forever, a musician. ☙

3

"CARVIN' THE BIRD"

CHARLIE PARKER'S DECISION to skip most of his high school classes did not make him an instant master of the alto saxophone. But that was not because he lacked the makings of a fine musician. For one thing, Parker possessed "a good ear"; he could listen to a song and easily understand its melody, shape, and structure. He also had a keen memory that allowed him to recall an entire tune after hearing it played only once or twice.

Yet there is more to being a musician than memorizing a melody. Amid his enthusiasm for playing the saxophone, Parker took some shortcuts in his musical education. In effect, he tried to utilize his natural talents without first acquiring a knowledge of music theory.

Learning how to play music is much like studying a new language. It is possible to master some phrases on one's own. But one cannot convey many ideas without a proper understanding of the rules that govern the language.

Musical compositions are always based in at least one key. (A key is the tonal center of a musical scale plus that central tone's six most closely related tones.)

A ladies' man even at age eight, Parker poses with a female friend near his Kansas City home. The youngster matured rapidly after moving from Kansas to Missouri in 1928 and finding himself just a stone's throw from the city's many nightclubs.

Shortly after Parker took up the saxophone, he made a point of studying the light, lyrical sounds of Lester Young, one of Kansas City's premier performers. "I was crazy about Lester," Parker said later. "He played so clean and beautiful."

When the notes to a melody are played in a specific key, a musician must know exactly which tones belong to that key, as well as the complementary tones, or harmonies, that will sound best with the melody. A musician must also recognize that the relationship between particular tones may shift as the composition proceeds from one key to the next. Any musician who does not possess this fundamental knowledge is limited in what he or she can play.

In 1934, Parker was already several years into his musical education and a member of the Deans of Swing. Nevertheless, he suffered from his lack of music theory. He would eventually acquire the necessary training; but until he did, his musical progress was slow.

Parker's real apprenticeship began when his mother took a job working nights as a cleaning woman at the local Western Union telegraph office. He had long been fascinated by the colorful nightclubs, dance halls, and saloons that he passed on his school route. The gambling, liquor, and loose women for which these night spots were known certainly appealed to the teenager. But it was the music that spilled out into the streets from almost every doorway that attracted him the most.

With no one at home to keep an eye on him, Parker would head out the front door shortly after his mother left for work. He would spend the night in and around the clubs that lined raucous 12th Street. Sometimes he came home very late; other nights he did not return at all. He listened and watched carefully as many of Kansas City's finest saxophonists, such as Herschel Evans, Budd Johnson, Ben Webster, and Lester Young, went about their nightly work.

At last, Charlie Parker was going to school again, although the classrooms were unlike any he had ever encountered. Attending this unique music school of nightclubs and cabarets almost every night of the week, he began to learn a tremendous amount about jazz, and about life in general. Young, bright, and very impressionable, he soaked it all up, absorbing everything that Kansas City's wild nightlife had to offer.

Soon Parker was looking and acting far more mature than his 14 years. As a result of his nighttime adventures, he lost whatever remaining interest he had in attending high school. A few months after his 15th birthday, he all but stopped going to his classes.

Parker played with the Deans of Swing for about a year and a half. The group finally broke up when most of its members graduated from Lincoln High and took on full-time jobs as musicians. Lawrence Keyes, the Deans of Swing's bandleader and pianist, managed to find the young saxophonist some work, as did Robert Simpson, the Deans' trombonist and Parker's best friend.

More than anyone else, Simpson encouraged Parker to continue practicing when most people found little to like in his playing. In fact, when Simpson was seriously ill with pneumonia and a heart ailment, he rose from his deathbed to persuade a bandleader not to fire Parker from the group. As always, the saxophonist was very grateful for his friend's show of loyalty. "To say that Charlie admired him is perhaps too mild," said Lawrence Keyes. "Charlie worshipped him and was in his company a great deal."

Simpson's death left Parker devastated, and he rarely allowed himself to grow close to anyone else in the years that followed. He once told a friend two decades later, "I don't let anyone get too close to me, even you. . . . Once in Kansas City I had a friend I liked very much, and a sorrowful thing happened. . . . He died."

One of the few people with whom Parker grew very close was Rebecca Ruffin, the daughter of Addie Parker's good friend Fanny Ruffin. Rebecca and her five siblings moved into the Parkers' house on Olive Street shortly after Fanny divorced her husband. Rebecca was Charlie's age, she also attended Lincoln High, and she was beautiful. One of the reasons why Parker had not dropped out of school completely was that, according to Rebecca, he enjoyed walking to and from Lincoln High with Rebecca and two of her sisters.

After the Ruffins moved in with the Parkers, Charlie and Rebecca were constant companions, acting like young couples do when they are courting. Two years passed before Fanny Ruffin decided that her daughter's relationship with Charlie had become "improper." Without a moment's hesitation, Fanny moved her family from the Parker home and forbade Rebecca to see her boyfriend.

The young couple continued to meet secretly, however, and several months later Charlie proposed to Rebecca. She accepted immediately and told her mother the news. Then she packed up her belongings and moved back into the Parkers' house.

Charlie Parker and Rebecca Ruffin were married the next day at the Kansas City courthouse. The bride was 16 years old. The groom was five weeks short of his 16th birthday.

Parker's marriage offered him little solace, however, from one of the bitterest episodes of his life. The incident had occurred at the Reno Club, one of Kansas City's most popular night spots. Housed in a long and narrow brick building on 12th Street, the club featured hour-long shows four times a night. In between shows, the house band played dance music for the customers.

Like most Kansas City cabarets, the Reno Club admitted both blacks and whites but was not racially integrated. Each race had its own dance floor, bar, and tables. Nevertheless, the club's atmosphere was usually relaxed and lively, until a jam session got underway. Then things became pretty heated.

The Reno Club was well known for its jam sessions. Musicians from all over the city would get together onstage, usually after their regular gigs, and play for their own enjoyment. Jam sessions have always been part of the jazz world, but in Parker's hometown they were like a rite of passage. When Kansas City musicians jammed, their freely improvised performances often turned into full-fledged battles—or, as the musicians referred to them, cutting contests. As in a knife fight, the goal was to "cut" your rivals, in this case by outplaying them.

Drummer Jo Jones unwittingly helped change the course of modern jazz by publicly humiliating Parker during a jam session at Kansas City's Reno Club in early 1936. "I went home and cried," the saxophonist remembered, "and didn't play again for three months." In the end, however, the incident prompted Parker to address his shortcomings as a musician—with spectacular results.

Jam sessions determined who was the better, the faster, the stronger, the more creative soloist. These musical wars proved to be the most demanding performances a musician would have to give, for no audience was as critical as a roomful of peers. Any musician was welcome to sit in, but those who could not make the grade immediately lost everyone else's respect.

Leading the Reno Club session one night in early 1936 was Jo Jones, the revolutionary drummer of the Count Basie Orchestra, Kansas City's finest jazz group. Another participant, also from the Basie band, was Lester Young, whose light, swinging tones would soon change the sound of the saxophone in jazz. Young was Parker's idol, and the teenager never missed an opportunity to hear, and learn from, the master.

This particular night, however, Parker had not arrived at the Reno Club merely to listen. He had been practicing constantly and had progressed a bit from his early days with the Deans of Swing. He had worked repeatedly on several tunes in preparation for this, his big night at the Reno Club, and he felt confident that he could hold his own. After all, he had played in other, less stellar jam sessions, with fair results.

The Reno Club was full; almost all the best musicians in town were there. One after another, they took their solo turn on the bandstand. Sixteen-year-old Charlie Parker waited and waited until it was finally his turn to play.

The makeshift band's rhythm section set a furious tempo as Parker began his solo. He started weakly, gained a little confidence, and ran through the musical phrases he had practiced without distinguishing himself, but without making any glaring errors either. The wise thing for the young saxophonist to have done would have been to play a single chorus and get off the bandstand before he ran out of ideas and embarrassed himself. There would be no great shame in a young musician taking a brief turn in the spotlight and then turning the stage over to the older, more skilled performers who were awaiting their chance to play.

Unfortunately for Parker, his ambition and enthusiasm won out over his better judgment. He began a second chorus and soon ran into trouble. He faltered badly, falling behind the band's rapid rhythms, and then exhausted his limited arsenal of practiced musical phrases. Spent and confused, and completely lost in the music, he struggled to continue playing. Meanwhile, laughter and cruel remarks had begun to rain down on him.

Finally, Jones lifted a cymbal from its stand and dropped it with a deafening crash near Parker's feet. Just as the losers were "gonged" on the "Major Bowe's Amateur Hour" radio program, Parker had been brought to a halt by Jones. Raucous laughter and catcalls descended on the teenager from every corner of the Reno Club. He had been humiliated in front of the cream of Kansas City's jazz community, and he had nobody but himself to blame.

Furious, Parker left the Reno Club as the derisive laughter and insults followed him out the door. "I'll fix those cats," he later told Gene Ramey. "Everybody's laughing at me now, but just wait and see."

Angry and more determined than ever, Parker set off to do just as he had vowed. He finally admitted to himself that he must compensate for the shortcomings in his formal music education. For one thing, he had never learned that music was played in different keys; he had merely assumed that all music was written in one common key. Parker asked Lawrence Keyes to explain about keys and other basics of music theory. Grasping the concepts quickly, the saxophonist went off to practice in solitude what he had just learned. It would be several months before he returned to the Kansas City nightclub scene.

Parker decided that his first task would be to learn all the notes in all 12 major keys. Relatively few keys were then being used in jazz; as a result, much of what he practiced was unnecessary. He did not know this, however, so he systematically learned to play the scales in each key, practicing each for hours and hours, until he knew them inside and out, then progressing to the next key and doing the same thing. He also began to experiment with harmonies and modulations (changes from one key to another in midsong), learning which combinations sounded best. Slowly, painstakingly, he began to understand the structure of music.

Parker also tried to improve his sound on the alto saxophone by trying different types of reeds, the vibrating slivers of wood that fit in the saxophone's mouthpiece and produce the sound when the player blows into the instrument. A saxophonist's sound is determined in part by the shape and hardness of the reed, the embouchure (the position and use of the lips around the mouthpiece), and the patterns of air that are exhaled into the instrument. First, Parker tried to imitate the sound of his idol, Lester Young. Later, he would imitate other Kansas City saxophonists until he had mastered the elements of their playing styles, too. Finally, he began to develop his own distinctive sound.

Parker's hard work began to offer results. By the end of 1936, he had made great strides in mastering his craft. Charlie Parker was now ready to perform in public. ❧

4

"COOL BLUES"

CHARLIE PARKER'S MUSICIANSHIP improved so greatly during his months of seclusion that he decided in November 1936 to resume his professional career. He felt it would be best, however, if his return to the music scene did not take place in Kansas City. Accordingly, he accepted a gig with drummer Ernest Daniels's band, which was scheduled to perform in a resort town in the Ozark Mountains resort region 150 miles east of Kansas City.

On a bitterly cold Thanksgiving Day, Daniels and his musicians set out in two cars for their evening engagement in the Ozarks. Both vehicles were speeding along a mountain road when the car in which Parker was riding hit a patch of ice, skidded off the roadway, and overturned several times before coming to a stop. George Wilkerson, the group's bassist, was killed; Daniels and Parker, the automobile's two other passengers, were seriously injured. The 16-year-old Parker suffered several broken ribs and a fractured spine, but he was lucky; he had been riding in the back seat of the car with the instruments wedged around him, and they had protected him from the full brunt of the collision.

Parker was in great pain by the time he returned to Kansas City, yet he refused to go to a segregated hospital. Instead, he went home and had his wife and his mother nurse his injuries. It took him two months to recuperate.

Parker at 16, an age when the budding saxophonist was spending most of his free time listening to Kansas City's finest jazzmen perform. "The joints were running full blast from nine P.M. to five A.M.," he recalled. "Usual pay was a dollar and twenty-five cents a night."

Parker launched his professional career just as Kansas City swing was gaining a national following. Andy Kirk and His Twelve Clouds of Joy, with whom Parker toured briefly in 1942 and 1944, was a leading practitioner of this lively jazz style.

Parker's accident brought one pleasant result. When he was finally well enough to leave his house, he received a surprise in the mail: an insurance company had awarded him several hundred dollars in compensation for his injuries. Parker immediately took a taxicab to a local music store. There he used the insurance money to purchase a new alto saxophone, one that had been manufactured in France by the Selmer Company, makers of the world's finest saxophones. For the first time in his life, Parker had something other than a shoddy instrument on which to perform. It boosted his self-confidence to own such a beautiful piece of equipment. With it, he was able to concentrate more fully on perfecting his playing.

Healthy and armed with a new saxophone, Parker lied about his age and joined the local musicians union. (Eighteen was the minimum age for membership, but Parker, always tall and husky, easily passed for two years older than he actually was.) As a member of the union, he soon landed a job with saxophonist Tommy Douglas's combo, which had steady engagements in the Ozarks.

The bandleader was a middle-aged, well-trained musician who had enjoyed a long and varied career. Douglas was hardly a major innovator, but he was an experienced professional, and he taught the teenaged Parker a great deal about harmony and improvisation. A terrific instructor, Douglas did much to improve Parker's playing technique in the few months that they performed together.

In the spring of 1937, Douglas was compelled to disband his group, which meant that Parker was again without work. The young musician managed to earn a little money by landing an occasional gig, often in the Ozarks. At the same time, he acquired a new habit, one that would haunt him for the rest of his life.

Alcohol and marijuana had long been part of the Kansas City jazz scene, and Parker had become intimately familiar with both substances by the time he had reached his mid-teens. After trying them, he began to experiment with an even more powerful stimulant, the amphetamine Benzedrine. Finally and most regrettably, in 1937 he turned to heroin and became addicted to the potent narcotic.

Parker's personality began to change after the start of his heroin addiction. Always a happy-go-lucky young man, he grew moody and unpredictable. Sometimes he would mistreat his wife and his mother; other times he would steal household items and pawn them so he could purchase more heroin. The drug soon caused his behavior to become so erratic that he would be irresistibly charming and amiable one moment and cruel and manipulative the next. Raised as a "mama's boy," he had always been a bit selfish. But when he became a heroin addict, the unpleasant aspects of his character became much more pronounced.

Drugs were not the sole cause of Parker's unsettled behavior. Many of his dark moods stemmed from a deep anger that grew from other sources. Frustration over the difficult life of a jazz musician, with its long hours, low pay, and frequent periods of unemployment, accounted for some of his feelings of resentment. So did his observations and experiences about race.

No matter what Parker achieved in his life, he believed that his black skin would always make him a second-class citizen. He might create absolutely brilliant music, but to white America it would be nothing more than low-class music. He would never merit much attention or win any lasting respect.

Because Parker was raised in a nation where legalized segregation was firmly in place, he had little reason to believe that W. E. B. Du Bois, A. Philip Randolph, Walter White, or America's other leading civil rights activists would succeed in changing the way blacks were treated by white society. The battle to end racial discrimination seemed a hopeless fight. And so Charlie Parker remained an angry young man, easing his wounded dignity and pride with a powerful and numbing narcotic.

It was a somewhat jaded Parker who went to work in the summer of 1937, performing occasional gigs with the bands of Lawrence Keyes and George E. Lee. Fortunately, there was a lot for him to gain from these two groups. Both bands boasted experienced musicians, and these veterans gave Parker valuable lessons in harmony and improvisation. With

Bandleader and saxophonist Buster Smith hired Parker as a second alto in 1937, then worked closely with him for more than a year, teaching the teenager about rapid-fire bursts of notes and other musical feats. "After a while," said Smith, "anything I could make on my horn, he could make too—and make something better out of it."

their help, he evolved into a highly accomplished saxophonist.

On his own in between jobs, Parker worked hard to add more polish to his playing style. Before his solo practice sessions, he would listen to the latest recordings of the Count Basie Orchestra. He would then teach himself Lester Young's tenor saxophone solos from the records, practicing each piece over and over on his alto saxophone until he could play it note for note. Not surprisingly, Parker's music during this period began to sound much like Young's.

The Count Basie Orchestra was then the most popular swing band in the United States. William ("Count") Basie had first brought the Kansas City–based musicians to New York City in 1936, and they began recording regularly in January 1937. By midsummer, the group had garnered a large following and almost singlehandedly turned Kansas City–style jazz into a national phenomenon.

Large jazz bands had been popular since the early 1920s, but Basie's group was different from previous orchestras. Its smooth rhythms, featuring four equal beats to each measure, defined the swing era, a period of high-spirited music that encouraged energetic dancing. The orchestra's success was also driven by several outstanding soloists in addition to Lester Young—trumpeter Buck Clayton, tenor saxophonist Herschel Evans, and trombonists Dicky Wells and Benny Morton—as well as vocalists Jimmy Rushing and Billie Holliday.

A few other Kansas City–style bands, such as Andy Kirk and His Twelve Clouds of Joy and Harlan Leonard's Kansas City Rockets, also gained a nationwide following. As a result, several Kansas City bandleaders put together large bands, featuring 12 to 16 musicians, to take advantage of the vogue for Kansas City–style jazz. The professorial-looking alto saxophonist Buster ("Prof") Smith was one of these bandleaders, and in the latter half of 1937 he hired 17-year-old Charlie Parker as the second alto for his new band.

Earlier in the decade, Buster Smith had been a member of the legendary Blue Devils, one of the most popular territory bands to tour the Southwest. He had also played briefly with Basie. Like Tommy Douglas, Smith was more of a polished professional than a stylistic innovator. Yet he possessed a distinctive approach to the alto saxophone, playing it with a lighter, less romantic tone than did the most popular alto players of the day: Johnny Hodges of the Duke Ellington Orchestra and Benny Carter.

Smith also included flurries of fast playing in his solos. He built these brief bursts around sixteenth notes (notes whose duration is one-sixteenth as long as a whole note). At the time, it was unusual for a soloist to play in this manner.

Smith taught these techniques, and much more, to Parker. The bandleader recognized the teenager's emerging talents and did all he could to encourage the young saxophonist, including sharing solo opportunities with him. "In my band, we'd split solos," Smith recalled. "If I took two, he'd take two; if I took three, he'd take three; and so forth. He always wanted me to take the first solo. I guess he thought he'd learn something that way. He did play like me a bit, I guess. But after a while, anything I could make on my horn, he could make too—and make something better out of it."

Parker performed with Smith first in a 12-piece band, then in smaller combos, with only four or five other members. All told, Parker played with Smith for more than a year. During that time, they developed an extremely close personal relationship. "He used to call me his dad," Smith said, "and I called him my boy."

By 1938, Smith's protégé was no longer regarded as a joke among Kansas City jazzmen; he had become a respected musician. Smith thought well of him, too, and he felt confident that he could line up an engagement for Parker and the other band members in New York City. Bidding his musicians good-bye, Smith traveled east to scout for business opportunities for them. Although he did not meet with any success, he decided to remain in New York on his own.

Back in Kansas City, Smith's group disbanded as soon as its musicians learned that their leader was not going to return. Once again, Parker had lost a father figure. And he was also without a steady job. ❧

5

"HOOTIE BLUES"

CHARLIE PARKER SPENT most of 1938 working in a variety of musical jobs in the Kansas City
area, including some dates with pianist Jay McShann,
who had performed with the teenaged saxophonist in
Buster Smith's group. Meanwhile, Parker continued
to build his reputation as a musician. He even wrote
some striking and creative arrangements for the house
band at a nightclub in the Kansas City suburbs where
he worked for several weeks. But he failed to land a
steady job and often went weeks without a gig.

At the start of the decade, it had been relatively
easy for a musician to find employment in Kansas
City. But a wave of political and social reform
had recently swept through, driving from power the
regime that had allowed the city's wild nightlife to
flourish. During the reform movement, numerous
clubs, saloons, and dance halls were shut down,
which eliminated jobs for many musicians. Some of
them followed the example of Count Basie and Andy
Kirk, who had moved their bands to New York to
take advantage of the greater commercial opportunities there.

Parker remained in Kansas City. His wife, Rebecca, had given birth to a son, Francis Leon Parker, in
January, and it was up to Charlie to support his
growing family. Unfortunately, the baby's arrival
could not save a failing marriage. The young couple
argued frequently, and the disputes occasionally grew
violent. Like his father, Charlie showed little interest

*Already a highly talented per-
former at age 20, Parker rehearses
with bassist Gene Ramey during
their tenure with the Jay McShann
Orchestra. "When I look back,"
Ramey said, "it seems to me that
Bird was at that time so advanced
in jazz that I do not think we
realized to what a degree his
ideas had become perfected."*

in being a good husband. His career kept him out of the house most nights, and he would often stay out past dawn even when he was not working. Apparently, Charlie saw other women on those occasions when he disappeared from home.

To make matters more difficult, Parker's mother and his wife had learned of his drug habit. Both women were horrified by their discovery and begged him to stop, but their pleadings did nothing to discourage the headstrong young man. Parker continued to steal household items and sell them for drug money. Eventually, even Addie's patience for her son's behavior began to run out.

Meanwhile, Parker was growing more and more disgusted with the scarcity of jobs in the Kansas City area. When an argument with a cabdriver escalated into a full-fledged fight—Parker nicked the driver with a knife and then received a brief jail term for his assault—it became obvious that the saxophonist needed a change of scene. He pawned his instrument and jumped on a freight train headed for Chicago.

Parker arrived there in November 1938, just ahead of the city's famed winter winds. Tired, hungry, broke, and without a saxophone, he went immediately to a "breakfast dance," a jam session held during the breakfast hours, at the 65 Club. According to singer Billy Eckstine, who saw the young saxophonist enter the club, Parker was "the raggedest guy you'd want to see."

Parker knew some of the musicians at the 65 Club from their days in Kansas City. After observing the proceedings for a while, he went up to one of them, Goon Gardner, and asked, "Can I come up and blow your horn?" "Go ahead," said Gardner, handing his alto saxophone to Parker, who immediately climbed onto the bandstand and joined the jam session. He played so beautifully, recalled Eckstine, that "he upset everybody in the joint."

Parker, however, did not stay in Chicago long enough to take advantage of the big impression he had made. Gardner took Parker to his own home, lent him some badly needed clean clothes and a clarinet to play until he could get a new saxophone, and helped him find a few short-term jobs. But within a few weeks, without a word of warning or explanation—not to mention gratitude—Parker pawned Gardner's clarinet and used the money to buy a bus ticket to New York City.

As soon as Parker reached Manhattan, he went directly to Buster Smith's apartment and arranged to stay with his former mentor until he could get settled. It took Parker a while, however, to find any gigs to his liking. His growing reputation in Kansas City and his brief triumph in Chicago meant nothing on the East Coast, where he was a complete unknown. He had to establish himself all over again, and this time in New York, where the jazz scene was bustling.

At first, Parker found only low-paying jobs. The better gigs were reserved for members of the local musicians' union, and it took several months to get a union card. Parker's youth also worked against him; many people were not willing to hire an 18-year-old saxophonist. As a result, he accepted the few short-term engagements he was offered. And whenever he could, he participated in late-night or early morning jam sessions for a few dollars or a free meal.

Desperate for money, Parker was eventually forced to take a job that had nothing to do with music; it was one of the few times in his life he would do so. For nine dollars a week, he washed dishes every night at Jimmy's Chicken Shack, a Harlem night spot. It was dull and depressing work, but the job did have one major benefit. Art Tatum was the featured pianist at Jimmy's.

Parker—and many other young musicians—had already been greatly impressed by Tatum's ornate

Parker received an advanced education in musical improvisation while listening to Art Tatum perform nightly at a Harlem cabaret in 1939. The pianist's mastery at varying basic melodies impressed the saxophonist so greatly he could not bring himself to speak to Tatum during the three months that they both worked at the jazz club.

improvisations. The nearly blind pianist possessed a keen musical mind that constantly explored new variations on basic melodies. His rapid shifts in key and tempo were breathtaking. As much as Parker hated dishwashing, he remained at Jimmy's for three months so he could listen to Tatum at the keyboard. Parker held the pianist in such awe, in fact, that he never spoke to Tatum the entire time they both worked at the restaurant.

Whenever Parker had the opportunity, he would jam with other young musicians at Clark Monroe's Uptown House in Harlem and apply the "lessons" he had learned from Tatum. Guitarist Biddy Fleet, one of the musicians at Monroe's, rehearsed frequently with Parker, answering his questions and helping him develop some of the progressive ideas suggested by Tatum's music. Parker was already hearing a new type of improvisation in his head, but it was a struggle for him to produce these ideas on his saxophone. Finally, during one of his practice sessions with Fleet in December 1938, he experienced a breakthrough.

Every melody can be supported by chords, which are groups of notes at fixed intervals that provide harmonic support for the melody. The chords used by most jazzmen in the 1930s contained notes that were three, five, and seven notes on the musical scale away from the note in the melody. "I'd been getting bored with the stereotyped chord changes that were being used at the time," Parker remembered, "and I kept thinking that there's bound to be something else. I could hear it sometimes but I couldn't play it."

On that December night, while jamming on the upbeat pop song "Cherokee" with Fleet, Parker succeeded at last. "I found," he said, "that by using the higher intervals of a chord as a melody line and backing them with appropriate related changes, I could play the thing I'd been hearing." Instead of using notes that were three to seven notes away from

the note in the melody, he substituted notes that were nine, eleven, or even thirteen intervals from the note in the melody. With that discovery, he recalled, "I came alive."

By stringing together these further-removed notes, Parker had created a new melody based on the same intervals as the original melody. "Cherokee," for example, could now have countless new variations, each original and distinct, but with a basis in the original tune. It was a discovery that differed enormously from previous jazz improvisation and would slowly lead to a revolution in the jazz world.

While Parker was beginning to explore the possibilities suggested by his discovery, he took a brief job with a group in Maryland. There he received a

Parker (third from left) joined the Jay McShann Orchestra in 1940 and remained in charge of the saxophone section for nearly two years, his longest stint with any band. He had first teamed up with Jay McShann (at the piano) a couple of years earlier, in Buster Smith's group.

telegram from his mother stating that his father had been stabbed to death. Using the train ticket that she wired along with the telegram, Parker returned at once to Kansas City for his father's funeral.

Rather than head back to the East Coast, Parker chose to remain in Kansas City, where he joined Harlan Leonard's Rockets, one of the city's most popular bands. Working closely with the Rockets was composer and arranger Tadd Dameron, who would become one of bebop's first great writer/arrangers. Like Parker, Dameron held progressive ideas about jazz, and they became friends.

Parker quickly established himself as a valued member of the group and was featured in a solo each night on "Cherokee," which gave him the chance to showcase his new ideas. But he did not get along very well with Harlan Leonard. The bandleader in turn grew weary of the saxophonist's frequent tardiness and fired him after about a month.

Fortunately for Parker, his friend Jay McShann, who had been the pianist in Buster Smith's group, was putting together his own big band. McShann was an amiable man with a well-known affection for *hooch*, a slang term for liquor; in fact, he bore the nickname Hootie, another slang word that meant being drunk. Nowhere near as strict as Leonard, McShann greatly respected Parker's talents and put him in charge of the band's saxophone section.

According to McShann, he gave Parker this appointment because the teenager had stopped using heroin. It is more likely, however, that Parker merely had his addiction under control for a short period. In any case, he was a model of professionalism when he joined forces with McShann. He diligently rehearsed and supervised the saxophone section, contributed arrangements and compositions to the band's repertoire, and was the Jay McShann Orchestra's most frequently featured soloist.

Although Parker was highly respected by his fellow musicians, his innovative approach to jazz was not always appreciated by the audiences. His solos sounded very different from those played by anyone else; to listeners accustomed to the smooth sounds of swing, Parker's music seemed unmelodic and incomprehensible. Whereas Johnny Hodges, Benny Carter, and the other leading alto saxophonists of the swing era produced a lush, full sound, Parker's tone, in comparison, was aggressive and harsh. Because the Jay McShann Orchestra's other altoist, John Jackson, played in a style more like Hodges and Carter's, his solos were better received by most listeners and dancers than Parker's were.

Unpopular with most audiences, Parker was not faring any better in his domestic life. When he returned to Kansas City, he went back to his wife, but it soon became clear that the differences between them had grown too great. At the end of 1939, he asked her for and was granted a divorce. Afterwards, Rebecca and Leon, then almost two years old, continued to live in the Olive Street house with Addie Parker.

Around the time of the divorce, Parker acquired the nickname by which he would become widely known. There are several stories as to how the name Yardbird—sometimes shortened to Yard, more frequently to Bird—came about. Whatever version is true, Parker apparently liked Yardbird and was known to use it when referring to himself.

One version is that Parker loved to eat chicken (which was sometimes called yardbird because the bird often ran loose in a yard). According to McShann, whenever Parker saw chicken on a menu he would say, "Give me some of that yardbird." The more popular story is that as the group was traveling to a performance, the car in which Parker was riding hit a chicken. Rather than see the bird go to waste,

The first recorded examples of Parker's playing emerged from this late 1940 studio session in Wichita, Kansas. Performing with the 20-year-old saxophonist (third from right) were (from left to right) trumpeter Buddy Anderson, drummer Gus Johnson, saxophonist Bob Mabane, trumpeter Orville Minor, Gene Ramey, and Jay McShann.

he ordered the driver to stop. Parker then got out of the car, scooped up the killed chicken, and insisted on bringing it to the band's destination, where it could be cooked and eaten. After that, the band members teasingly called him Yardbird.

Parker apparently enjoyed his tenure with the Jay McShann Orchestra, for he stayed with the group longer than he did with any other band. The orchestra toured the Midwest, South, and Southwest continuously in 1940 and built up a significant following through performances and live radio broadcasts. The band was not the most talented or the most creative on the scene, but its members played with an undeniable energy that proved popular with dancers and listeners. Walter Brown, a singer with a bluesy tenor voice, was one of the group's major assets.

Parker, however, was the orchestra's most valuable player. "Cherokee," the song on which he first realized his idea of a new approach to jazz improvisation, was the Jay McShann Orchestra's best number and one the band members never tired of playing. They constantly rehearsed and refined the tune, and Parker's nightly solo on the song always proved to be a work of spontaneous genius. Even though audiences did not always understand or appreciate the brilliance of his solos, there was little question among the band's members that, aside from McShann, Bird was the group's heart and soul. They recognized him as their most talented member and, as the resident practical joker, the source of much of their fun.

The Jay McShann Orchestra, recalled one of its members, Gene Ramey, who had also played with Parker in the Deans of Swing, "was the only band I've ever known that seemed to spend all its spare time jamming or rehearsing. We used to jam on trains and buses; and as soon as we got into a town, we'd try to find somebody's house where we could hold a session. All this was inspired by Bird, because the new ideas he was bringing to the band made everybody anxious to play."

In November 1940, the band was playing a weekend engagement in Wichita, Kansas. A jazz fan who also managed a local radio station arranged for a small group of musicians from the orchestra to come to the station and make some informal recordings. These records were not intended for sale to the public; they were supposed to be sold only to other radio stations. Whether they were ever broadcast, in Wichita or elsewhere, is unclear. In any event, they were kept in private hands for almost 35 years, until they were finally released to the record-buying public. They remain the first recorded examples of Parker's playing.

On these recordings, the music is entertaining but hardly unique. It sounds a bit like Count Basie or Andy Kirk's recordings from the same period. One aspect makes it different: the solos of Charlie Parker. Featured on all seven songs, his playing demonstrates a strong Lester Young influence, yet he is clearly moving into new musical territory.

Parker's solos on these records possess an energy that was uncommon for 1940: he sometimes uses harmonic ideas that point toward the music that

The label for the Jay McShann–Charlie Parker composition "Hootie Blues." Released by Decca in 1941, the song was one of the first tracks ever recorded by the Jay McShann Orchestra.

would be called bebop a few years later, and the rapid-fire flurries of notes that would soon become his trademark are also in evidence. Confident and well constructed, and clearly the most interesting element of these performances, Parker's solos offer a fascinating glimpse of a musical genius who was just coming to grips with his revolutionary abilities. At the time of the recording, he was just 20 years old.

The Jay McShann Orchestra continued its constant touring into the early months of 1941. The group had already developed a sizable following when, in April, it was finally given the opportunity to make some records. Decca Records recorded the band in Dallas, Texas. Once again, Parker was prominently featured on most of the tracks. His solos on "Swingmatism," an instrumental, and "Hootie Blues," which also featured Walter Brown, are brilliant, revealing impressive developments in just the few months since the Wichita recordings.

Musicians who heard these records were greatly impressed, although some of the older players disliked Parker's tone, which struck them as harsh and discordant. Predictably, the record-buying public found Brown's vocals more interesting, and the songs that featured him were the most popular recordings the McShann band made. Parker did not solo on most of Brown's numbers, nor did he receive much solo space when the orchestra recorded in Chicago in November and in New York in July 1942. By the latter date, the band's recordings had begun to sell well, and the group was ready to move into New York City's big-time music scene.

The Jay McShann Orchestra may have been riding high when its successful engagement at Harlem's Savoy Ballroom kicked off in the summer of 1942, but Parker was growing frustrated with the band's direction. Vocals were entering more and more into the performances, thereby limiting his own solo opportunities. In addition, audiences still did not seem to appreciate his innovative style, certainly not in the way his peers did.

Eager to pursue his own playing style outside the somewhat rigid confines of a big band, Parker discovered a growing number of young musicians who appreciated his artistry and shared some of his progressive ideas. Kenny Clarke, Dizzy Gillespie, and Thelonious Monk were among the "young lions" applying the basic ideas of bebop to the swing style of jazz that had been popular for almost a decade. They would meet nightly at various Harlem clubs to share their musical discoveries and theories and jam until dawn.

Minton's Playhouse, on 118th Street, and Monroe's Uptown House, on 138th Street, were the two most popular gathering spots for these young beboppers. Some of the older, more established swing musicians visited these late-night sessions. Confident and aggressive, the beboppers did not hesitate to challenge and conquer the swing musicians who chose to take part in the jam sessions. The beboppers were fiercely competitive; Minton's especially was *their* turf; and outplaying musicians who were once their idols was all part of the game. The beboppers' goal was not to coexist with swing but to replace it. Some of the older musicians embraced the new jazz form; others left the clubs either angry or fearful over the shift that was taking place.

In August 1942, McShann announced to his band members that the orchestra was leaving town and returning to Kansas City. Upon hearing the news, Parker decided that the time to make a change in his career had arrived. He let McShann know that instead of going back to Kansas City, he would be staying in New York to pursue his future.

6

"ORNITHOLOGY"

CHARLIE PARKER LEFT the Jay McShann Orchestra at an unfavorable time. In the spring of 1942, just a few months after the outbreak of World War II, the U.S. government began to ration all materials necessary for the war effort that were in short supply. Gasoline and rubber tires were among the products to fall into this category, and their rationing effectively curtailed all forms of long-distance travel, including the touring of jazz bands.

The war years brought one other significant change to the music world. The American Federation of Musicians (AFM), the labor union to which all professional musicians belonged, went through a long dispute with the nation's three major record companies: Columbia, Decca, and Victor. Each of these companies refused the AFM's request to increase the royalty payments made to recording artists based on the number of records that were sold. The AFM responded in August 1942 by forbidding its members to make records for any of the three companies.

The AFM strike effectively shut down the entire recording industry, for the Great Depression had put virtually every other record company out of business. One of the unfortunate results of the recording ban was that the early development of bebop almost went undocumented. Although bebop represented a revolutionary change in the direction of jazz, it did not immediately replace swing. Instead, bebop-oriented musicians began to be featured in some of the swing-based bands that performed in New York

A flock of Bird-watchers listens closely to Parker as the saxophonist performs with a small ensemble. He was the most important jazz soloist since trumpeter Louis Armstrong.

City. Most of these hybrid groups never had the chance to cut records, however, because the AFM recording ban lasted for a year against Decca; Columbia and Victor did not reach an agreement with the union until 1944.

A number of small record companies came into existence and tried to fill the void during the recording ban. Consequently, Dizzy Gillespie, Thelonious Monk, and a few other bebop pioneers were able to make records on their own or with more-established artists. For the most part, though, the transitional steps in the change from swing to bebop were not captured on disk. And without these intermediate stages, the first bebop records, which were released in 1944 and 1945, seemed even more revolutionary than they really were.

Parker was among the musicians who never received the opportunity to record. This key period in his musical development, during which the concepts he and his fellow beboppers had nurtured and shaped finally came together, would exist only in the memories of those who had the chance to hear him perform in person. By all accounts, the music was remarkable. "Everybody was experimenting around 1942," recalled clarinetist Tony Scott, "but nobody had set a style yet. Bird provided the push."

After leaving the Jay McShann Orchestra in August, Parker spent much of the rest of 1942 participating in the jam sessions at Minton's Playhouse and Monroe's Uptown House. Occasionally he played dates with McShann; he also appeared briefly with Andy Kirk's band. But try as he might, Parker could not find steady work.

He made inquiries into joining the Count Basie Orchestra, but his addiction to heroin kept Parker from getting the job. Toward the end of his regular employment with McShann's orchestra, his dependence on heroin had increased. By the time he left

the band, his addiction had become severe, and he was less dependable than ever before.

The saxophonist's life away from the music scene had become just as disorganized. He had no real home; he survived by relying on the generosity of fellow musicians and other friends. Finally, a group of them ended this period of frustration and relative inactivity by finding Parker a job with a big band led by pianist Earl Hines.

Like Basie, Hines was a leading figure in the jazz world. He had collaborated on Louis Armstrong's groundbreaking recordings of the late 1920s, then went on to lead his own successful orchestra during the 1930s and into the following decade. Hines applied Armstrong's revolutionary improvisation technique to the piano, embellishing a melody with his own spontaneous creations. By late 1942, Hines, although not yet 40 years old, was one of jazz's elder statesmen.

The piano-playing bandleader had heard Parker perform with McShann some months earlier and had been impressed. The saxophonist in fact had ap-

Like a pair of musical bookends, Parker (far right) and trumpeter Dizzy Gillespie (far left) jam with the Earl Hines Orchestra during an April 1943 appearance at New York City's Apollo Theatre. Parker left the group at the end of the year after becoming bored with the orchestra's music. "Charlie had a photographic mind," recalled Earl Hines (sitting at the left piano, opposite Sarah Vaughan). "When we would rehearse a new arrangement, he would run his part down once, and when we were ready to play it the second time, he knew the whole thing from memory."

proached Hines about joining his band, but at the time there were no openings in the saxophone section. The situation had changed by December, yet there was one catch. It was Budd Johnson, the group's featured tenor player, who was leaving and needed to be replaced; the band already had the requisite number of alto saxophones. To join Hines's orchestra, Parker would have to switch from alto to tenor saxophone.

Parker had never really studied the larger, lower-voiced tenor saxophone. But he had played the instrument before, and so he gladly accepted Hines's offer. Parker, however, did not own a tenor—in fact, he was playing a borrowed alto at the time. Hines went out the next day and bought a saxophone for his new tenor.

If Parker was hoping to join a steady, stable group of musicians, this job fit the bill. The Earl Hines Orchestra was nationally known and toured more than most groups did during the war years. But if Parker's desire was also to join an innovative band, he soon realized that Hines's orchestra was nothing of the sort. It was a big band that played sophisticated arrangements of swing-style jazz. In addition to Hines on piano, the group featured two vocalists: Billy Eckstine and the stunningly talented Sarah Vaughan. Then only a teenager, Vaughan would soon establish herself as one of the greatest singers in the history of American popular music.

For his part, Parker was spotlighted as a soloist on several numbers. As he did with the Jay McShann Orchestra, he influenced a change in the band's sound. But this time he had help. The Hines orchestra's personnel included several musicians who were part of the bebop movement, including Dizzy Gillespie and trumpeter Little Benny Harris.

Hines, Gillespie recalled, "had a lotta young guys who all wanted to play in the modern style." On occasion, these band members would race through a composition. "We'd get to swinging so much," said Vaughan, "Dizzy would come down and grab me and start jitterbugging all over the place." Hines appreciated the talents of these young musicians, but he was not willing to adopt their style of music, and he suppressed their influence as much as he could. And so Parker slowly grew disenchanted with the group.

No commercial recordings exist of Parker's work with the Earl Hines Orchestra because of the recording ban. But in the friendly and relaxed environment of a Chicago hotel room, Bob Redcross, a friend of Eckstine's, made some private recordings of Parker, Gillespie, and a few other musicians. These recordings, with Bird on tenor saxophone and Dizzy on trumpet, offer a rare opportunity to hear bebop's founding geniuses developing their craft.

While not as striking as the fiery, passionate music Parker and Gillespie would make later on, these hotel-room recordings reveal both young men playing for their own amusement, challenging and prompting each other. All told, the Redcross recordings present a classic example of two great musicians demonstrating their uncanny creative rapport. Little more than a rumor for many decades, the recordings were not discovered until the mid-1980s, when they were released to the public.

In 1943, while the Hines band was in Washington, D.C., Parker was married for the second time, this time to Geraldine Scott, a dancer. Their marriage was as unsuccessful as Parker's first attempt at matrimony, and the couple split up after about a year. It appears, however, that they were never legally divorced.

Toward the end of 1943, after Parker had spent about eight months with the Earl Hines Orchestra, he quit the band. His continuing drug addiction had

Leader of the world's first bebop big band, vocalist Billy Eckstine (right) pays close attention to two of his orchestra's stars, Dizzy Gillespie (left) and Parker. "The whole school would listen to what Bird would play," Eckstine said. "He was so spontaneous that things which ran out of his mind—which he didn't think were anything—were classics."

caused him to miss many of the group's performances, which had infuriated Hines. Meanwhile, Parker had become bored with the orchestra's music, which was exactly the dull and predictable type of jazz he and the other beboppers had been rebelling against.

Leaving the Earl Hines Orchestra along with Parker were Gillespie, Eckstine, and several of the younger musicians. Their plan was for Eckstine, who was already popular with the public, to form a band that featured his singing and the writing, arranging, and playing of the beboppers. The musicians went their separate ways while arrangements for the new band proceeded. Parker returned to Kansas City to visit his mother and spent a short time playing local gigs. He then spent the spring of 1944 touring with two different orchestras, Andy Kirk's and Noble Sissle's.

In the meantime, Eckstine had begun to assemble his band, which featured Vaughan in addition to the young beboppers. Gillespie, who served as the musical director, was elated over the group Eckstine was putting together. "We were playing bebop, the modern style," the trumpeter said. "No other band like this one existed in the world." By the time Parker joined the orchestra in mid-1944, it had already been together long enough to have made a few recordings for minor record labels.

Parker served a dual role with the band. He was its featured alto saxophonist and the leader of the reed section, which made him responsible for rehearsing the other saxophonists and getting their playing to mesh with that of the other musicians. Parker performed brilliantly with the Billy Eckstine Orchestra, but once again he did not find his stay satisfying.

For one thing, the group was not commercially successful; even though the recording ban had practically ended, opportunities to make records, which in turn helped promote a band, remained rare. In addition, the Billy Eckstine Orchestra's progressive instrumentals still sounded new and strange to many audiences, who found it difficult to appreciate the music. "It was," said Redcross, the band's road manager, "the first dance band that ever played that people couldn't dance to."

Eckstine's orchestra had its share of minor successes. But Parker continued to exhibit the erratic behavior that had plagued his stays with both McShann's and Hines's bands; he was frequently tardy for or altogether absent from the group's performances. Apparently, he felt stifled by the format of any big band, even one that reflected his own musical ideas.

By the end of August 1944, Parker had told Eckstine that he was leaving the band. He returned to New York City with the intention of pursuing his ideas in the less restrictive structure of a small group.

7

"NOW'S THE TIME"

T HE HEART OF the jazz world in 1944 was a stretch along New York City's 52nd Street, between Fifth and Seventh avenues, that was known simply as the Street. Almost every night, large and appreciative audiences filled the Downbeat, the Onyx, and the dozens of other small clubs and bars that lined this two-block strip, eager to hear singer Billie Holiday, trumpeter Oran ("Hot Lips") Page, saxophonists Coleman Hawkins and Ben Webster, and the many other talented performers who had become stars during the swing era. Loud and wild, the Street's many cabarets were a magnet for fun seekers, troublemakers, and jazz fans, many of whom were eager to escape from the concerns and sacrifices of World War II.

In addition to the good times that the Street promised, it was one of the few public places where blacks and whites could mingle without encountering any racial hostility. In most cities and towns across the United States, nightclubs and bars were still racially segregated. Some establishments that catered to white customers even recalled the great jazz clubs of the 1920s and 1930s in featuring black entertainers while excluding black patrons.

That was not the case on 52nd Street. "Generally there were few problems of racial discrimination in the clubs on 52nd Street because most of the bands there were black," recalled Dizzy Gillespie. "Even among the clientele on 52nd Street there was very

One of the few orchestra leaders who managed to keep a big band intact during the rise of bebop, Duke Ellington (left) considered hiring Parker, until the saxophonist told the popular pianist and composer how much money he wanted to be paid. "Bird," Ellington reportedly said, "for that kind of dough I'd work for you."

little racist feeling. That was the one spot in New York where there was very little racist feeling."

Charlie Parker arrived on 52nd Street at the end of the summer of 1944. By then, a growing number of listeners had become interested in bebop, and club owners were discovering that they could make money by promoting the new jazz style. No longer would bebop be confined to a brief solo within a traditional swing performance, as it had been for most of the period since Parker's emergence with the Jay McShann Orchestra. The time had arrived for bebop to assume a major role in jazz.

Even though Parker had quit the Billy Eckstine Orchestra without making any records with the group, his performances as a leading soloist with the band had attracted attention. As a result, he found for the first time in his life that his services were in great demand.

Parker eventually decided to join a quintet led by Ben Webster, the talented tenor saxophonist who had been a featured soloist in the Duke Ellington Orchestra during the early 1940s. A decade older than Parker and primarily influenced by Coleman Hawkins, Webster was not a bebopper and initially did not like the new style. According to Eckstine, who had been at Minton's in 1943 when Webster first heard Parker, the older saxophonist went up to the bandstand and snatched the tenor saxophone out of the younger musician's hands, telling him, "That horn ain't supposed to sound that fast."

Later that night, however, Webster went around telling everyone, "I heard a guy—I swear he's going to make everyone crazy on tenor." But Webster was only half right. Parker preferred the alto saxophone and seldom played the tenor after leaving the Hines band.

When Parker was between sets with Webster's group, he could often be found sitting in with other

The first club to present a small ensemble that played only bebop, the Three Deuces (far right) was among the dozens of New York City night spots that made 52nd Street a mecca for jazz fans. According to bebop pioneer Dizzy Gillespie, "The height of the perfection of our music occurred in the Three Deuces with Charlie Parker," where the two friends shared the stage from the fall of 1944 to early 1945.

musicians at various clubs along the Street. During one of his breaks, he jammed with guitarist Tiny Grimes, who also harbored ambitions of becoming a professional singer. Their conversation soon led to Parker's next recording session. Grimes had been asked to record two vocals and two instrumental tracks for a small company, Savoy Records; he invited Parker to take part in the session.

The two vocals performed by Grimes's quartet are pleasant but unexceptional, with brief, interesting contributions from Parker. The saxophonist was prominently featured, however, on the two instrumentals, "Red Cross" and "Tiny's Tempo." Named (in spite of the spelling error) for Bob Redcross, "Red Cross" was arguably Parker's first extended opportunity to display his abilities in a recording studio. The song was loosely based on George and Ira Gershwin's pop standard "I Got Rhythm," and the quartet's arrangement was as much swing as bebop.

Nevertheless, Parker's contributions were outstanding. He dominated the quirky ensemble passages that opened and closed the tune, and his exciting solo employed the rapid-fire phrases that would soon become his trademark. All told, the recording amply demonstrated Parker's ability to use a simple set of chord changes as the springboard to an inventive and unpredictable improvisation. The Grimes vocals received little attention from the public, but musicians and bebop fans soon discovered both "Red Cross" and "Tiny's Tempo," and Parker's stature in the jazz world rose even higher.

Meanwhile, Parker was on the move again. Leaving Webster's quintet after only a few weeks, he and Gillespie were hired in the fall of 1944 to lead a small ensemble at the Three Deuces, one of the many night spots on 52nd Street. Along with bassist Ray Brown, drummer Max Roach, and Bud Powell, they made the Three Deuces the first club to feature a group that played only bebop.

Parker and Gillespie's engagement at the Three Deuces was a magical experience for almost everyone who attended the shows. Some of the listeners were still bewildered by bebop, finding it aggressive, non-melodic, and undanceable. And several influential music critics who preferred New Orleans–style jazz and swing took great pleasure in attacking bebop in their reviews. But the majority of the crowds that came to hear the quintet perform at the Three Deuces understood that something new and exciting was taking place and were thrilled to witness bebop's flowering into an important musical form.

Parker and Gillespie's partnership was certainly among the most exceptional in American music history. Both were largely responsible for developing and popularizing bebop, and each man regarded the other as his closest musical collaborator. "I guess Parker and I had a meeting of the minds," Gillespie said, "because both of us inspired each other." On the bandstand, they offered one another support and competition while displaying remarkable rapport. Both musicians later admitted it was when they played together, at the Three Deuces and elsewhere, that each of them produced the greatest performances of his career.

Like Parker, Gillespie, who was three years older than the saxophonist, had served a long apprenticeship in swing-oriented big bands. He had found these groups to be as limiting and frustrating as Parker did, but rather than turn to drugs and alcohol as a means of diversion, he escaped from the dreary routine by exercising his sharply developed sense of humor. Gillespie's wild antics, in fact, had earned him the nickname Dizzy when he was 18 years old and just launching his professional career.

Gillespie had much more than playfulness going for him. He was handsome, charming, and stylish. And he often used the latest slang, or jive, in his speech, a habit that would soon be noted by the press and imitated by his many fans. Most important of all, he was a well-trained musician.

Gillespie played the piano as well as the trumpet, and his sophisticated musical compositions and arrangements revealed a form of genius shared by few in the jazz world, including Parker. As a trumpeter, Gillespie was influenced above all by swing trumpeter Roy Eldridge. But it did not take long for Gillespie to become one of the most distinctive and original trumpeters jazz has ever produced, and he was always looking for new challenges.

After years of performing with musicians who insisted on playing swing, Gillespie was thrilled to be working in a small group with a bandmate who created modern jazz as well as Parker did. "The height of the perfection of our music occurred in the Three Deuces with Charlie Parker," Gillespie wrote in his autobiography, *To Be or Not to Bop*. "Yard and I were like two peas. Our music was like putting whipped cream on jello. His contribution and mine just happened to go together, like putting salt in rice. . . .

Trumpeter Dizzy Gillespie was Parker's closest musical collaborator and one of the few jazzmen who could keep up with the constant flow of ideas that poured out of Bird's saxophone. "He'd play other tunes inside the chords of the original melody," Gillespie remembered, "and they were always right."

Sometimes I couldn't tell whether I was playing or not because the notes were so close together."

As close as Bird and Dizzy were musically, they were extremely different away from the spotlight. Despite his zany and energetic stage personality, Gillespie stressed punctuality for gigs and recording sessions and was the epitome of responsibility in his dealings with club owners, managers, agents, and recording company executives. Unlike Parker, he was a smart businessman and made a good living from his music; in 1951, he even founded his own record company.

In his personal life, too, Dizzy was not at all like Bird. Calling Lorraine Willis "the anchor that I need," Gillespie wedded the chorus-line dancer in 1940 and has remained married to her ever since. He deliberately avoided using heroin, which he saw ruin the lives of Parker and many other young musicians. And he never let problems in his personal life affect his music—unlike Parker, who could be moody both on- and offstage and did not care who knew about it.

When Parker and Gillespie were not working together, they remained friendly but not particularly close. "My closeness to him was mostly musical," Dizzy recalled. "I didn't hang out with the same people he hung out with. I didn't do the same things he did. . . . Yard always denied he was doing [drugs] to me. I never *saw* him use anything. All I saw were the symptoms."

Onstage, things were very different; everything clicked. The tunes that Parker and Gillespie performed were generally their own compositions, which were based on the chord changes of popular songs. Rearranging the chord patterns of tunes such as "I Got Rhythm" and "Cherokee" could produce numerous variations, each substantially different from the next. In fact, the original tune underlying a variation would often be unrecognizable to all but the most knowledgeable listener.

Much of Bird and Dizzy's music rejected the steady, even beats of swing and relied on breaks in rhythm to create a powerful dramatic effect. Many of their numbers also featured catchy and unusual beginnings and endings, soon to become a common characteristic of bebop. (Among the first wave of beboppers, only Gillespie and Thelonious Monk proved capable of creating many strikingly original compositions that were not derivative of other songs. Of the dozens of songs credited to Parker over the course of his career, there were just a handful that could not be traced to an earlier song.)

Parker and Gillespie were known to play a lot of up-tempo songs, often at blistering speeds, as if to show off the tremendous dexterity and energy they each possessed. On these tunes, they seemed to be staging a battle rather than a performance. Although to most listeners it seemed as if each musician was reading the other man's mind, the precision they displayed in their arrangements could only be produced by many hours of practice and rehearsal.

Parker and Gillespie were equally capable of playing slower, melodic songs. Their emotional improvisations on ballads revealed another side of their abilities amid the display of bebop's characteristic harmonies. As fiery and aggressive as their up-tempo tunes could be, Bird and Dizzy demonstrated an unusual sense of grace and beauty in their ballads.

For the remainder of 1944 and into 1945, Parker and Gillespie continued their engagement at the Three Deuces, drawing appreciative crowds that often included other young musicians who were attracted to the bebop movement. Sometimes after Bird and Dizzy left the Three Deuces, they would hide their instruments under their coats and visit another club on the Street. "In the middle of a tune, they'd

Shortly after Dizzy Gillespie (right) and Parker ended their gig at the Three Deuces in mid-1945, they teamed up once more for a pair of concerts at New York City's Town Hall. Marking the first time bebop was ever featured in a concert hall, the enthusiastically received shows helped modern jazz gain more respect in the music world.

slip up on the stand" where Coleman Hawkins or Illinois Jacquet might be playing, recalled trumpeter Duke Garrett, "and eat them up."

In early 1945, the two virtuosos finally had the chance to record with a few other jazzmen, under Gillespie's leadership, for a small record label called Guild. The first true bebop recordings, the Guild sides offer stunning and timeless music that displays Bird and Dizzy at the height of their powers. Tunes such as "Groovin' High," "Shaw Nuff," and "Hot House"— all Gillespie compositions that had been featured at the Three Deuces—found an audience with progressive-minded jazz fans and thereby enabled the sounds of bebop to spread across the nation.

Parker and Gillespie's gig at the Three Deuces ended a short time after they made these recordings. In mid-1945, they returned to the stage as the Gillespie-Parker Quintet, performing two concerts at a larger venue, New York City's Town Hall. These appearances, which marked the first time bebop was ever featured in a concert hall, left the critics dazzled. In fact, the words of praise that followed the concert were sufficient to convince Gillespie that he should pursue his long-standing ambition of forming a big bebop-playing band. It would feature his own compositions and arrangements as well as those of the other new talents who had arrived on the jazz scene, including Tadd Dameron and Gil Fuller.

Parker had no interest in returning to the big-band format, even if it meant playing modern-style jazz. He remained on the Street, leading his own quintet at several clubs. No longer in the shadow cast by Gillespie's unique personality, Parker finally received the recognition he deserved. Jazz fans and fellow musicians realized that he was perhaps the greatest improviser ever. There was a constant flow of ideas from his saxophone as he explored the countless variations of a song's chords. When Parker soloed, he was essentially composing spontaneously, weaving new melodies from the basic elements of the tune. Many jazz musicians had done this before, but only Louis Armstrong had approached Parker's talents as an improviser.

The full scope of Bird's abilities, however, was recognized only by other musicians and a relatively small group of fans and critics. The complexity of his music was beyond the grasp of casual listeners, who wanted to be entertained, not challenged or provoked, by the music they paid to hear. And Parker was unwilling at this point in his career to dilute his music to reach a larger audience.

That attitude carried into his manner onstage. Parker was a bright and articulate man, but his stage personality lacked the crowd-pleasing antics of a Dizzy Gillespie. As a result, Bird did not attract the widespread attention that Dizzy had gained and would continue to receive. Destined to remain more a cult hero than a popular star, Parker resented the perception held by many that Gillespie was bebop's creator and greatest talent. Unfortunately, his resentment would turn to bitterness and would last for most of his remaining years. ❧

8

"CHASIN' THE BIRD"

CHARLIE PARKER CONTINUED to lead his own ensemble on 52nd Street for much of 1945. Whereas the general public remained largely unaware of his musical abilities, a small but dedicated group of appreciative fans began to follow every development in his career. The combination of Parker's groundbreaking music and his rebellious, elusive personality created a mystique about him, and his followers soon proved to be the most dedicated in the jazz world.

A good number of these fans were women. Somewhat on the pudgy side and not particularly handsome, Parker nevertheless possessed an expressive face and a warm, boyish smile that many members of the opposite sex found irresistible. In 1945, he formed serious—and simultaneous—involvements with two women, Doris Sydnor and Chan Richardson, each of whom he would eventually live with, as though they were husband and wife. But these two relationships did not keep him from pursuing numerous romantic flings with the women who flocked to the clubs where he performed.

Meanwhile, Parker continued to have virtually no home life. He slept little, often staying away from

"The beat in a bop band is with the music, against it, behind," Parker said. "It helps it. Help is the big thing. It has no continuity of beat, no steady chug-chug. Jazz has, and that's why bop is more flexible."

his New York City apartment for several days at a time. After a night of carousing, he would show up at a friend's doorstep just before daybreak and ask to come in, whether he was welcome or not.

Perhaps it was Parker's doting mother who had laid the groundwork for his habit of taking advantage of others. Or maybe his father sowed the seeds of irresponsibility. Whatever the case, Parker borrowed money from friends, family, and fellow musicians, as well as from total strangers, and rarely paid them back. Sometimes he even failed to give his musicians their agreed-upon salaries because he had already spent all or part of their money.

Acquaintances would put themselves out for Parker because he possessed the joyous and loving nature he had displayed so readily as a child. Generous to a fault, he spent freely on himself and others when he was earning a good income. To Parker's way of thinking, money was meant to be enjoyed, and it did not matter if it was his or someone else's.

Nightclub owners were among the people who discovered just how irresponsible Bird could be. Because he spent money quickly, he often demanded that a good portion of his salary be paid in advance. Then, on a later date, he would look around the crowded club and demand additional compensation from the owner.

Parker believed, often correctly, that the salary he had been paid was a trivial sum compared to the profits his employer made. Like most jazz musicians of the time, especially those who were black, he was treated like a second-class laborer and earned a decent wage only by working every night, sometimes in hostile settings. The lowly plight of a jazz artist disturbed Parker more than it did most of his peers, and he became increasingly dependent on heroin as an outlet for his frustrations.

Parker also responded by becoming manipulative and destructive. If a club owner refused to give him more money, Parker would argue and complain. Sometimes he would take his revenge by running up large drinking and dining bills and refuse to pay them when his engagement ended. Other times he would vent his anger by showing up late for each evening's sets. When he finally did appear, his immense musical skills and a modest amount of charm often caused everyone to forgive his tardy arrival. To many observers, the nickname Bird seemed appropriate for a man whose music took jazz soaring to new heights yet who seemed to travel through life as carefree as a creature of flight.

In late November 1945, Parker finally had the opportunity to record with a band under his own leadership. The ensemble featured the talented young rhythm section of drummer Max Roach and bassist Curley Russell. The trumpeter was 19-year-old Miles Davis, recently arrived from St. Louis and still developing his musical skills. Dizzy Gillespie, under contract with another record company, was not allowed to participate openly in the recordings, at least not on trumpet. He played the piano on four songs and snuck in to play the trumpet on the stunning "Ko Ko."

"Ko Ko" was a variation of Bird's old showpiece, "Cherokee," and it ranks as one of the classic performances in jazz history. An explosive torrent of ideas offered at a breakneck pace, "Ko Ko" is the culmination of all the musical theories Parker had developed since he began his career. The interplay at the beginning and the end between Parker and Gillespie (on trumpet) is complex and precise. Dizzy offers simple but effective support on piano to Bird's astounding solo, and Roach demonstrates that in bebop the drummer is a frontline instrumentalist, freed from

In November 1945, a few months after Parker formed his first ensemble, he held a recording session with his own group. Trumpeter Miles Davis (right) filled in for Dizzy Gillespie on most of the numbers and subsequently began to perform with the saxophonist on a regular basis.

the simple timekeeping chores of swing drumming. "Ko Ko," less than three minutes in length, still serves today as an impressive résumé for bebop, a demonstration of its full power and achievement.

The recording session, which was released by Savoy Records, produced two other outstanding tunes, "Billie's Bounce" and "Now's the Time." Both have become regarded as jazz classics. While they were not big hits, Parker's recordings for Savoy further exposed him to jazz fans and musicians across the country.

Meanwhile, the Dizzy Gillespie Orchestra had been traveling throughout the South, attempting to interest the region's large black population in the jazz world's new sound. The tour, billed as Hepsations 1945, proved to be a commercial failure and broke up within a matter months. People had come to the shows expecting to hear music they could dance to; finding bebop too difficult to comprehend, they booed Gillespie's big band and stomped out of the music hall. "They wouldn't even listen to us," Gillespie complained.

Seeking a friendlier setting, Gillespie rejoined Parker on 52nd Street. By then, however, the Street's heyday had already begun to pass. Some of the club owners had been forced to close their doors because of an increase of vice and rowdiness in the area. Billy Shaw, Gillespie's manager, began to look for a better business opportunity for his client and found one at a Los Angeles night spot owned by Billy Berg. The engagement would make Gillespie's quintet the first bebop band to perform in California. There was only one catch to the deal: Parker had to be a member of the group.

By this point in their friendship, Gillespie knew all too well how unreliable Parker could be and was reluctant to include him in the quintet. As a precaution, Gillespie brought along a sixth musician, vibraphonist Milt Jackson. If Parker was late for a performance or failed to appear, the band would still have the five members that its contract with Berg required.

Because there was not much work to be found on 52nd Street, Parker agreed to join the entourage, but he was not eager to make the trip. He had grown tired of Gillespie's crowd-pleasing antics and believed that such behavior was demeaning and unnecessary. "The leopard coats and the wild hats are just another part of the managers' routines to make him box office," Bird said of Dizzy. Apparently, Parker also resented the fact that Gillespie continued to receive most of the attention from critics and audiences.

Fortunately, neither Parker's nor Gillespie's reservations interfered with the opening performance at Billy Berg's. The club was extremely crowded that night; it seemed that every jazz musician and fan in California was in attendance. Few on the West Coast had heard the music of Parker, Gillespie, or the other beboppers: Milt Jackson, Ray Brown, pianist Al Haig, and drummer Stan Levey. But their New York performances had already become legendary. The arrival of Parker and Gillespie was the biggest event on the Los Angeles jazz scene in years.

Characteristically, Parker missed the evening's first two sets in their entirety. The third set also began without Bird on the bandstand. But as Gillespie and the other four musicians started to play "Cherokee," the music onstage was joined by the faint sound of an alto saxophone coming from the rear of the club. Gradually, the sound of the saxophone grew louder, as Parker approached the bandstand, tossing off one sharp musical phrase after another. He was in full musical flight by the time he reached the stage.

Parker proceeded to dazzle the attentive audience for the rest of the evening. With this dramatic entrance and subsequent rousing performance, he was introduced to the California jazz scene. The people in the crowd were very impressed by their first taste of live bebop, and Parker in particular gained many new fans.

As terrific as the initial response was on opening night, the size of the audience at Billy Berg's began to dwindle only a few days later. The less adventurous listeners who came to hear Parker and Gillespie were perplexed by the music, much as the first New York audiences had been. In the weeks that followed, only a small number of music lovers came to the nightclub.

Parker showed up for most of the sets at Billy Berg's. By all accounts, the band played brilliantly, with Bird and Dizzy continuing to inspire each other to new musical heights almost every night. Live recordings of the band that were made during its California stay rank among the most exciting that Parker and Gillespie ever made. But as the engagement neared its scheduled end in early February 1946, there was no discussion of extending the band's contract.

A week before the engagement concluded, Parker and Gillespie took part in a Jazz at the Philharmonic concert that featured some of the biggest names of the swing era. Among the other musicians onstage was Parker's idol from his Kansas City days, Lester Young, still gifted but a changed man, his playing showing the immense psychological damage caused by his terrible experiences in the U.S. Army, when he had been court-martialed and imprisoned in a stockade after he was caught smoking marijuana. Parker and Gillespie performed well at the concert and won new listeners in an audience that included more swing than bebop fans.

The following week, as his quintet played its final sets at Billy Berg's, Gillespie made arrangements for the band members to head back to New York. When it came time to depart for their flight, Parker could not be located. Gillespie and the rest of the group returned to the East Coast without the wayward Bird, who had cashed in his plane ticket and had disappeared onto the mean streets of Los Angeles.

It is unclear why Parker chose to remain in California, a part of the country he hardly knew and did not really like. What made his decision even more curious was that heroin was far harder to come by in Los Angeles than in New York. The powerful narcotic was not only very expensive and difficult to find on the West Coast, but whenever Parker managed to purchase it, the drug was often of poor quality. Unable to obtain on a regular basis the heroin his body craved, he often suffered the painful effects of withdrawal, the symptoms of which left him physically sick, haggard-looking, and in a precarious mental condition.

Perhaps Parker remained in California because he felt the need to place some distance between himself and Gillespie, and pursue his own career far from his former partner's long shadow. Given his dependence on heroin and the severe damage that his addiction was causing him physically and mentally, it is probable that he did not fully consider the disadvantages of remaining in Los Angeles. In any event, he took a gig headlining at the Finale Club, a gathering place for the city's beboppers, and led its house band for several months.

Parker's income from the Finale Club was modest compared to his earnings on 52nd Street and at Billy Berg's, and his strained finances made it even more difficult for him to buy the heroin he desperately desired. As his health problems worsened, he was fortunate to have a friend like Miles Davis to help out. The trumpeter had followed his idol to the West Coast by taking a gig with the Benny Carter Orchestra, a Los Angeles–based band that was on its way back to California. As soon as it reached Los Angeles, Davis began sitting in with Parker after the trumpeter had finished his evening's work with the Benny Carter Orchestra. Finally Davis left Carter's band to play full time with Bird.

Trumpeter Howard McGhee, a talented bebopper who had known Parker since the days when they both played in big bands, was another loyal and protective friend who sought to help the troubled saxophonist. McGhee and his wife invited Parker to move in with them, and they generally kept an eye on him at a time when he could hardly take care of himself.

Even so, Parker's physical and mental deterioration continued. His addiction to heroin was by now completely out of control. Because he could not

Parker takes a break at Billy Berg's Los Angeles nightclub in early 1946. The 25-year-old saxophonist's physical and mental condition continued to deteriorate during his first West Coast trip, until he suffered a nervous breakdown on July 29 and was committed to Camarillo State Hospital.

always get hold of the drug, his body regularly suffered the horrors of withdrawal. The strain that Parker was inflicting on himself clearly took its toll. The once plump musician looked extremely thin and much older than his 25 years. Meanwhile, his erratic behavior was typical of a person on the brink of a mental collapse.

Amazingly, Parker continued to perform as often as he possibly could and was still capable of producing terrific music. Ross Russell, a record store owner who had just founded a record company, met Parker and arranged for him to lead a recording session for Russell's new label, Dial Records. On March 28,

Russell assembled many of Los Angeles's finest young beboppers in a recording studio to back Parker. It was to be one of his greatest sessions.

On this day, Parker was physically well and arrived at the studio on time and prepared to play. Two Parker compositions, both of which referred obliquely to himself—the beautiful, haunting "Yardbird Suite" and "Ornithology"—were among the five tunes recorded. Another fine number, "Moose the Mooche," was named after Parker's drug dealer in Los Angeles. These three confident and original compositions were soon regarded as jazz classics. Even though Dial Records was just a small company and its products were not widely distributed, the Parker recordings made a huge impact. Those who heard them could not ignore Parker's immense talents, and he again gained more fans as a result.

Although the Dial recordings offered continued evidence of Parker's growth as a musician, there were more trying times ahead. The Finale Club closed, and Parker had difficulty finding regular work. While his income shrank, he spent all of what he did earn on heroin or, when none was available, cheap wine.

On July 29, four months after his first Dial recording session, Parker returned to the recording studio. Unfortunately, he was in desperate need of heroin and arrived at the studio a hyperactive and confused man. "Bird was really disturbed," remembered McGhee. "He was turning around and around, and his horn was shooting up in the air, but the sound came out fine. There were no wrong notes, and I feel that the records are beautiful."

Compared to the cuts of the March session, the music recorded in July is painfully emotional, particularly the ballad "Lover Man," which would become a hit record. Parker's playing is indeed beautiful, as McGhee described it, but the music is that of a weary and defeated man who can no longer hide the agony he feels in his soul. The contrast to his bold and confident March recordings is striking. Later on, when "Lover Man" was released by Dial, Parker became furious with Ross Russell. The saxophonist hated the music from the session—it was as if it reminded him of the immense pain he was feeling at the time of its recording.

Only hours after recording "Lover Man," Parker returned to the rundown hotel where he was living. By then, he was in an extremely agitated state, and he caused a disturbance in the hotel's lobby. Then he returned to his room and somehow managed to start a small fire. No one was injured in the blaze. Nevertheless, the police were summoned and took the raging Parker into custody.

This time, Parker had gotten himself into more trouble than even he could handle: he had suffered a nervous breakdown. Without his consent, he was committed to Camarillo State Hospital, an institution for the mentally ill. ❦

9

"RELAXIN' AT CAMARILLO"

Getting Himself Committed to Camarillo State Hospital, where he was placed under constant medical supervision, probably saved Charlie Parker's life. Far removed from the street life that had worn him down for so long, the 26-year-old received intensive psychiatric care and managed to break his long dependency on heroin and liquor. He ate nutritious meals regularly and got a solid amount of sleep every night. His once-robust physical health soon returned; for the first time in a long while, Parker looked and felt as young as he actually was.

Unlike many state-run mental hospitals in the mid-1940s, Camarillo was a relatively pleasant and well-operated institution. The patients received progressive and effective psychiatric treatment. They were also allowed to take part in constructive activities to pass the time; Parker chose to lead and play in the hospital's band and to work in the vegetable garden, a task he truly seemed to enjoy. Friends were allowed to visit him after several months, and they reported that he seemed happy, healthy, and relaxed.

Parker soon grew restless, however. Anxious to resume his musical career, he began to seek his release

Parker returns to the recording studio in early 1947, shortly after his release from Camarillo State Hospital. Joining him at the microphone are Dial Records owner Ross Russell (center) and vocalist Earl Coleman.

from the hospital, only to find it was not a simple matter, since he had been committed to Camarillo by the courts. His mental condition had to be evaluated by the hospital's physicians over a period of time. If his problems were deemed minor, then he could be released.

According to Ross Russell, Parker's doctors did not diagnose his dependency on heroin as the major cause of his troubles. Some of the doctors suspected he was suffering from the personality disorder known as schizophrenia; others believed he had merely demonstrated patterns of behavior that were not uncommon to the harsh, stress-filled life of many black Americans. This second group of physicians believed that Parker's immense musical abilities, which set him apart from others, would give him the incentive and opportunity to lead a normal and productive life, and they said he was not a major threat to himself or to society.

In the meantime, Parker's friends also worked to obtain his release from Camarillo. Doris Sydnor, one of the women with whom he had become romantically involved in New York, came to California as soon as she learned of Parker's hospitalization. Thereafter, she worked tirelessly with Russell to get Parker released, writing numerous letters to the doctors and administrators of the mental institution. They also organized a benefit concert to buy Parker a saxophone and clothing to replace those items he had lost in the fire in his hotel room.

Parker was finally released from Camarillo at the end of January 1947, after spending six months there as a patient. Feeling rejuvenated and ready to work, he participated in two recording sessions for Dial the following month. Due largely to his improved mental and physical states, these February studio dates, during which Parker produced such soon-to-be classics as "Cool Blues," "Cheers," and "Relaxin' at Camarillo," were far more productive than the traumatic "Lover Man" session held the previous July. A couple of weeks later, Parker began to work at the Hi-De-Ho Club in Los Angeles, appearing in a group with Howard McGhee.

Parker returned to New York at the end of March. It was more than 14 months since he had left his adopted city, and significant changes in the jazz scene had taken place during his absence. Bebop had gained greatly in popularity, with the new music now being featured at most of the city's jazz clubs. Without sacrificing any of its explosive energy or stylistic innovations, bebop had become commercially successful and had even begun to win the respect of the most doubting jazz critics.

Parker reaped one of the benefits of bebop's recent popularity. He discovered that his role as one of the music's founding fathers had earned him legendary status, even after his prolonged absence from the jazz scene. Dizzy Gillespie remained bebop's biggest star, but Parker was not far behind. He had gained another wave of fans through his California recordings for Dial, which had sold fairly well, and was greeted in New York by constant offers of work. Even more pleasing, he was able to command higher salaries than he had ever previously earned.

Parker soon put together a small group consisting of many of the best young musicians on the scene. Miles Davis, no longer a tentative newcomer but an emerging major talent on the trumpet, shared the spotlight with Parker. Max Roach, an extraordinarily inventive percussionist, anchored a rhythm section that also included pianist Duke Jordan and bassist Tommy Potter. This quintet remained together, without any substitutions, for almost 18 months, an unusual period of stability for Parker.

Parker and his group played their first gigs in April, at the Three Deuces. After that, they worked

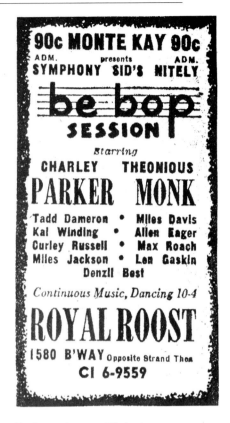

Parker and pianist Thelonious Monk, two of modern jazz's creators, are prominently featured in a June 5, 1948, newspaper advertisement for a bebop session at the Royal Roost in New York City.

steadily on 52nd Street and in the larger, newer nightclubs that had begun to spring up on nearby Broadway. Throughout this period, Parker was not using heroin regularly; and because he was no longer suffering from the wild mood swings that his addiction had caused, he was generally professional and responsible and produced music that was consistent and creative. He had plenty of help. Miles Davis was rapidly developing as a soloist, his cool and reflective trumpet playing serving as an effective contrast to Parker's more aggressive and emotional style. Rather than displaying the constant high-energy musical competition that had existed between Parker and Gillespie, the "fire and ice" styles of Parker and Davis complemented each other. Together, they produced music of great emotional range and depth.

Davis regarded playing in Parker's group as an invaluable period in his own musical education: "I was really happy to be playing with Bird again, because playing with him brought out the best in me at the time. He could play so many different styles and never repeat the same musical idea. His creativity and musical ideas were endless."

Another member of the band, Max Roach, echoed Davis's words of praise: "Bird was kind of like the sun, giving off the energy we drew from him. . . . In any musical situation, his ideas just bounded out, and this inspired anyone who was around. He had a way of playing that affected every instrument on the bandstand . . . even the way I play drums."

Parker seldom explained to the musicians what he wanted them to play. He expected them to pay close attention to his own playing and to intuitively find their own path in the music. This approach produced music that was occasionally sloppy and ragged, but it added spontaneity to the performance and encouraged the group's members to explore their own ideas. More than anything else, it was Parker's

A Parker solo astounds Miles Davis (second from right) during a 1948 performance with pianist Al Haig (far left) and Tommy Potter (far right) at the Royal Roost. Weekly broadcasts from the nightclub enabled the ensemble's music to reach thousands of radio listeners.

ability to teach by example that inspired musicians to work with him and enabled them to tolerate his long-standing irresponsibility with money and his reluctance to rehearse between performances.

A number of these musicians followed Parker into the recording studio. He had signed one contract with Dial and another with Savoy Records, in each case obliging himself to record exclusively with that company. As his popularity soared, both record labels brought him into the studio. Either company could have sued the other to protect its claim to Parker's recordings; but rather than get tied up in a legal battle, each company was content to have records to issue that had been made by bebop's rising star.

In 1947 alone, Parker recorded three sessions for each company, producing dozens of new titles. He made excellent music for both record labels, but his recordings for Dial are arguably the finest music of his career.

Savoy had a policy of recording only songs that had been written by the recording artist; all of the tunes had to be either original compositions or disguised versions of standard pop songs. Savoy thereby avoided paying the composer's royalties that it would have otherwise been obligated to pay. What was more, Savoy could claim the publishing rights to the composition and collect a sizable portion of the royalties that the new song earned, potentially a large sum of money in the case of a hit recording. This policy prevented Parker from recording some of his best performance material for Savoy.

Dial had no such policy, and so Parker was able to record the combination of originals and standard tunes he performed onstage. Ross Russell had followed Parker east to New York, and the sessions he arranged for the saxophonist captured the quintet's best material. The lively "Scrapple from the Apple," an imaginative rewrite by Parker of Fats Waller's "Honeysuckle Rose"; the swinging "Dexterity"; and "The Hymn," which alternates brilliant rapid-fire passages with hymn-like refrains, are the up-tempo highlights of the New York Dial sessions.

The real gems from these recording sessions, however, are the ballads. Parker's beautiful and expressive interpretations of these slow, melodic tunes demonstrate a restraint and maturity that was only hinted at in his earlier work. The directness and honesty of his ballad recordings reveal the gentle, romantic side of Charlie Parker, and they possess a stunning emotional power. "Embraceable You," "My Old Flame," "Out of Nowhere," and, most of all, "Bird of Paradise" (a thinly veiled variation of "All the Things You Are") are some of the most beautiful jazz recordings ever made. Parker built solos of stunning inventiveness and creativity from these familiar pop tunes; they demonstrate a perfect balance of improvisational genius and melodic virtuosity.

Parker made a rare appearance without his quintet on September 29, 1947, when he was the featured guest at a Gillespie concert staged at New York City's Carnegie Hall. The show, headlined by Dizzy's 15-

piece big band, broke an attendance record at the prestigious music hall. Both musicians played well before the adoring crowd, recapturing the glory of their days as bandmates several years earlier.

Near the end of 1947, Parker and his band traveled across the United States with the Jazz at the Philharmonic tour, sharing the stage with bop and swing musicians. Parker was one of the stars of the tour, and he was well received by audiences all over. He then took his quintet to Chicago, Detroit, Philadelphia, and Washington, D.C., for successful engagements in late 1947 and early 1948.

Around this time, the American Federation of Musicians started another recording ban that lasted into late 1948. As a result, Parker did not make any studio recordings from December 1947 until September 1948. Luckily, his performances at the Royal Roost, one of the big new jazz nightclubs on Broadway, were broadcast regularly on the radio. Some of his fans recorded these early morning broadcasts, and their transcriptions were released years later on long-playing records, cassettes, and, most recently, compact discs.

These fascinating recordings demonstrate Parker's uncanny ability to create and surprise on the bandstand. Some of the tunes were played nightly and therefore show up repeatedly on the recordings. Yet Parker's solos on these songs are always different; he seldom repeats himself, finding new variations even in tunes he has played hundreds of times. Freed of the time constraints of a studio recording, which limited performances to about three minutes, Parker and the band were able to take longer, more exploratory solos, with some tunes lasting five or six minutes.

After the recording ban ended, Parker held one last recording session for Savoy in September 1948. He then signed a lucrative contract with Mercury

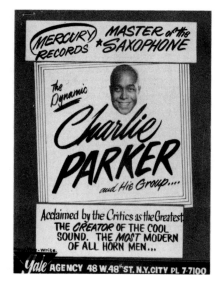

"I'm accused of having been one of the pioneers," Parker told downbeat *magazine in 1949, around the time that Mercury Records ran this advertisement heralding him as "the creator of the cool sound." He was, in fact, bebop's foremost innovator.*

Records, a much larger company than Savoy. He hoped a bigger company would help his music reach a larger audience and perhaps even get it to cross over to the huge pop music market that usually had a limited interest in jazz.

Meanwhile, Parker's quintet continued to work regularly at the Royal Roost in the fall and early winter of 1948. By Christmas Eve, however, Davis was ready to begin a solo career, one that would last for more than four decades. With Davis's departure, Parker's greatest band was no more.

Unfortunately for Parker, the quintet was not the only thing in his life that was about to come to an end. Offstage and away from the microphones, 1947 and 1948 had been relatively happy times for Parker. He had not only gained recognition for his talents but had experienced contentment in his private life.

Just as the personnel in Parker's quintet had remained constant during this period, so had his involvement with Doris Sydnor. A tall, shy woman who was extremely protective of him in an almost maternal way, she had not been a jazz fan before meeting him. In fact, Sydnor was one of the few women in Parker's adult life who was attracted to him for his personality rather than for his music. Totally devoted to the saxophonist, she offered him a stable home life, far removed from the destructive temptations that often lurked in the jazz world.

Parker and Sydnor eventually married in Mexico in late 1948. Unfortunately, as had happened to the saxophonist twice in the past, his marriage broke up, this time in less than a year. And once again, he was never formally divorced.

Parker's heroin addiction had become worse by the time of the failure of the marriage. He had tried to remain drug-free, but after he was back in the jazz world for a while, he began using heroin again. Clearly, he lacked the willpower to resist the drug.

What troubled the saxophonist most about his addiction was seeing many young musicians reach the false conclusion that if they wanted to play like the great Charlie Parker, they had to become heroin users. Parker actively discouraged all musicians—and the fans who idolized him—from using the narcotic. He recognized how dangerous and destructive heroin was, even if he could not control his own habit. He never, ever encouraged anyone to try the powerful narcotic, and on several occasions he threatened to beat up young band members if he found them experimenting with the drug.

"Any musician who says he is playing better either on tea, the needle, or when he is juiced, is a plain straight liar," Parker told *downbeat* magazine in 1949. "When I get too much to drink, I can't even finger well, let alone play decent ideas. And in the days when I was on the stuff, I may have *thought* I was playing better, but listening to some of the records now, I know I wasn't. Some of these smart kids who think you have to be completely knocked out to be a good hornman are just plain crazy. It isn't true. I know, believe me."

Nevertheless, a number of musicians, some of them gifted, others perhaps lacking in talent, felt that using heroin would enable them to play as brilliantly as Parker did. They were wrong. Bird played brilliantly despite heroin, not because of it. Only his immense musical abilities and unusual physical strength enabled him to overcome the drug's numbing effects when he played. Many careers were damaged or ruined as a result of heroin addiction, and Parker acknowledged on several occasions that he, as a role model for a generation of jazz musicians, was partially responsible.

10

"CELEBRITY"

B Y THE LATE 1940s, when Charlie Parker was several years into his stardom in the jazz world, he had earned an impressive following among knowledgeable fans. He was not a household name, and he would never gain that level of popularity during his lifetime. Among those who followed jazz, however, he was an artist whose work could not be ignored.

Parker's biggest fans seemed to be other jazz musicians because they alone had the musical knowledge to fully appreciate the complexity of what he was trying to accomplish—and how tremendously successful he was in his attempts. Not only did his revolutionary approach to rhythm and improvisation influence almost an entire generation of young artists, but his ideas found acceptance among musicians who had been stars since the 1920s and 1930s. A number of these performers had initially resisted bebop's influence; yet Parker's musical abilities eventually won their respect and admiration.

Bebop may have been slow to catch on at first, but when it did, Parker and the other beboppers took charge of the jazz world in a few short years. Older jazz styles kept their audiences. But by the late 1940s, the present and future direction of jazz clearly lay in the ideas that had arrived with bebop. To the surprise of some and the excitement of many, bebop had become the jazz establishment.

Parker gives a playful pat to drummer Max Roach backstage at the second annual Paris Jazz Festival in May 1949, as Swedish drummer Sven Bollhem looks on. Parker proved to be a tremendous success at the Paris concert, which marked his first performance in Europe.

Thoroughly enjoying the fruits of his success, Parker unwinds with composer and arranger Tadd Dameron (fourth from left) at a Paris nightclub in 1949. The 28-year-old saxophonist briefly entertained the thought of settling in France, after discovering that jazz artists were treated with much more respect in Europe than they were in the United States.

Like 1948, which held many triumphs for Parker, 1949 began with a large share of successes. The quintet's popular engagement and broadcasts from the Royal Roost continued into March. Talented trumpeter Kenny Dorham replaced Miles Davis, and pianist Al Haig, the first white musician to play with Parker on a regular basis, also joined the band. And then there was Parker's new recording contract with Mercury Records, which created the opportunity for his music to reach a larger audience, as well as a chance for him to make more money through increased record sales. Mercury could distribute and promote his records more effectively than the small labels for which he had previously recorded.

To protect its investment in an artist, a large record company such as Mercury generally maintained a high level of control over the recording

process. The label's staff often selected the backing musicians and material and closely supervised the recording sessions. The performer often had only limited influence in the planning and recording.

Such was the case with Parker at Mercury: he had less control over the form and quality of his music during these sessions than when he had recorded for the smaller companies. Unfortunately, this loss of control had a damaging effect on the caliber of his recorded music. The qualities that had made his earlier recordings so special were often obscured or absent in his work for Mercury.

For example, Parker's first Mercury sides, recorded in January 1949, paired him with a Latin jazz orchestra. It was an interesting experiment, but the results hardly rank among his more memorable recordings. Parker's initial small-group recordings for

Mercury, made in March and May of the same year, were indistinctive and uninspired.

In May 1949, Parker accepted an invitation to appear in France at the second annual Paris Jazz Festival. It was his first opportunity to work in Europe, where jazz had won an admiring, enthusiastic audience more than 30 years earlier. Unlike most Americans, who thought of jazz musicians merely as entertainers, Europeans regarded them as true artists, along the lines of composers and performers of classical music. And nowhere were American jazz musicians accorded more respect than in France, as Parker and his quintet soon discovered.

On the bill with Parker was a group with Miles Davis as its co-leader. Also featured at the Paris concert were performers who represented earlier jazz styles, such as soprano saxophonist Sidney Bechet, the New Orleans pioneer who was the first American jazz musician to gain stardom in Europe, and swing trumpeter Hot Lips Page, who had played with Count Basie's Kansas City band in the 1930s. The French audience offered a warm reception to all these jazz artists, and Parker's performances in particular were a tremendous success. Members of France's classical music establishment were among the most vocal in their praise.

Parker was surprised and moved by the affection and respect shown by the audience in Paris. He was further impressed when he met several black American jazz musicians who had emigrated from the United States and had settled in France. After listening to their stories of what it was like to live in a nation where they were respected as serious artists and where racism was less oppressive than in their native country, Parker considered leaving the United States and moving to France.

After weighing his options, Parker did not make the jump abroad. Still, his trip overseas left him with

an increased awareness of his stature as an artist, and as soon as he returned to New York he began listening to classical music and to talk about developing his own ideas for longer, symphonic works in a classical style. On several occasions over the next few years, he met classical composers, with whom he discussed approaches to musical composition. He also mentioned to his friends and fellow musicians that he was thinking about beginning formal studies of music theory with classical teachers and composers.

But Parker's ambitions of pursuing his musical studies never progressed beyond these discussions. Once he was back in New York, he fell into his customary and demanding routine of playing at night-

Bird with Strings: Parker makes his recording debut with a string orchestra in an effort to emphasize his more melodic and romantic side. Drummer Buddy Rich (far left), bassist Ray Brown (second from left), and Mitch Miller (second from right), playing the oboe, accompanied the saxophonist at this November 1949 Mercury studio session.

clubs. He also performed in several more Jazz at the Philharmonic concerts, both as a soloist in the shows' popular jam sessions and with his own group, which underwent a pair of personnel changes: Roy Haynes replaced Max Roach on drums, and Red Rodney, a young trumpeter from Philadelphia, succeeded Kenny Dorham.

For Parker, there was no escape from the degrading world of a black American jazz musician. "Though he was the idol of all musicians," bandmate Duke Jordan recalled, "Bird knew the limitations of his success and felt annoyed that he was confined to just playing in nightclubs. . . . Being a Negro, he could just go so far and no farther."

In November, Parker attempted to escape his confinement by going into the recording studio without his own band; a string orchestra accompanied him instead. The idea was to record Parker as the featured soloist on a series of ballads that would spotlight his more melodic and romantic side. It is unclear whether Bird with Strings was conceived by the Mercury Records staff, by Parker, or by both; but it seems that Parker was a willing participant in the project. He may have equated the orchestral settings and melodicism featured on these sides with the classical music with which he had recently become fascinated.

In any case, Bird with Strings, as a concept and as music, is neither jazz nor classical music. These orchestral arrangements are lush and pretty, yet they are also dull and conservative and anything but jazzlike. Parker's improvisations are brilliant and highly inventive; his solos, however, are the only jazz elements on these recordings, which were clearly designed to reach the popular music market. Perhaps in his quest for respectability and popularity, Parker believed that such recordings would gain him the acclaim he felt he deserved. If so, he was correct to the extent that many people heard him perform for the first time through the popular success of Bird with Strings: they proved to be the biggest-selling Parker recordings released during his lifetime.

Many jazz fans and critics, however, were horrified by Bird with Strings. They regarded it at the very least as a serious compromise of Parker's talents, if not a total betrayal of his position as a jazz revolutionary. In the end, the recordings seriously damaged his reputation as a leader in the development of modern jazz.

By the time Bird with Strings was recorded, Parker had separated from his third wife, Doris, and had resumed his relationship with pretty Chan Richardson, a former dancer and avid jazz fan. A single mother with a young daughter, Richardson still greatly admired Parker, whom she had dated before his ill-fated trip to California in 1945.

Richardson would remain involved with Parker for the rest of his life. They lived together for most of that time, and their relationship proved more stable and lasting than any of his three marriages. Although Parker and Richardson were never legally married—in part because he never divorced his second or third wives—she did change her name to Parker, and she provided him with a home life and much-needed emotional support in the trying times to come. All told, she seemed to understand Parker's complex moods and needs more completely than the other women who had played major roles in his life.

After resuming his relationship with Richardson, Parker saw his life take another upswing when Birdland opened on December 15, 1949. Although he had no part in the ownership of the club, he was pleased that the night spot had been named for him, and he was the headline act on Birdland's opening-night, all-star bill. In the months that followed, he played there frequently, both with his quintet and

Parker and his newest hornman, Red Rodney, take in a performance by bebop's premier trumpeter, Dizzy Gillespie (reflected in mirror). On a tour through the segregated South in 1950, Parker circumvented the law that barred blacks and whites from sharing a stage by insisting that the red-headed Rodney was actually a light-skinned black.

with the Bird with Strings orchestra. At the peak of his popularity and one of the major attractions on the New York jazz scene, Parker always drew large audiences to the sizable nightclub.

On Christmas Eve, Parker and his quintet took time out from their Birdland appearances to close out an all-star concert of modern jazz stars at Carnegie Hall. Red Rodney and Al Haig proved themselves outstanding accompanists and soloists at the concert, which was recorded live. But it was Parker's extended solos, particularly on the ballad "Bird of Paradise," that made the 1949 Carnegie Hall concert one of the greatest performances of his career.

The following year, as Parker continued to perform at Birdland and other New York City venues, the personnel of his group changed frequently, almost from gig to gig. Among the notable musicians who played with Parker were Bud Powell, one of the greatest of all bebop pianists, and Fats Navarro, a sensitive and original trumpeter whose heroin addiction led to his death from tuberculosis at age 26.

In 1950, Parker also traveled across the Midwest and South with his quintet and with the Jazz at the Philharmonic tour. He avoided a potential obstacle during his band's own tour of the segregated South, where it was not legally permitted for blacks and whites to share a stage, by claiming that Red Rodney, the group's red-haired, Jewish trumpeter, was a light-skinned black. To reinforce the idea, Parker referred to Rodney onstage as Albino Red and always asked the trumpeter to sing a blues song during each set. The shy, soft-spoken Rodney was hardly a vocalist, but he did the best he could, and no one seriously questioned his presence in Parker's group.

Parker also appeared in a number of Bird with Strings engagements in 1950. Attracted by the records, these shows drew large audiences; but the music was no more interesting in live performance than it had been on record. Parker and the orchestra had written musical arrangements for only a limited number of songs. As a result, the musicians were forced to play the same tunes the same way, night after night. There was no room for spontaneity or excitement.

Parker participated in two more Bird with Strings recording sessions and another encounter with a Latin jazz band during 1950. None of these studio efforts was outstanding. His best recordings of this period occurred with a small group that included Dizzy Gillespie and Thelonious Monk, another bebop creator as well as its most original composer. Bird and Dizzy are in top form, playing with the same fire and creativity they had shown five years earlier. The June 6 session produced six solid tunes, including the confident "Bloomdido" and a breakneck showpiece called "Leap Frog." This memorable session was nearly spoiled by the flashy and insensitive drumming of Buddy Rich, whose style was incompatible with Parker and Gillespie's. (The inclusion of unsuitable backing musicians is, unfortunately, a recurring problem with Parker's Mercury recordings.)

In November, Parker once again traveled to Europe, this time without his band. A concert tour had been arranged for him in Scandinavia, where he was to be accompanied by a group of Swedish beboppers who, if not as talented as their American counterparts, were more enthusiastic about their music. As in Paris the previous year, Parker received a tremendous welcome. In fact, he had a grand time in northern Europe, jamming or partying whenever he was not performing.

Unfortunately, Parker consumed a large amount of the drugs and alcohol that were provided to him by well-meaning but misguided European fans. Staying up night after night, he failed to get adequate rest and grew increasingly worn as the visit continued. After performing in Denmark, he headed to Paris, but before a scheduled concert he began to experience severe stomach pains. Too ill to perform, he flew home to New York.

The pain was caused by the stomach ulcers that Parker had been suffering from for several years. In addition to the ulcers, he had also developed a heart condition. Using heroin regularly did not help either ailment, nor did the way he overindulged in his intake of food and alcohol. For years, he had shown a general lack of concern for his health, continuing to overeat, drink too much, and use heroin even though it caused damage to his heart. At last, his wayward habits had begun to take their toll. He was only a few months past his 30th birthday, yet his physical condition had deteriorated to the point where his body was more like that of a much older man.

In an effort to reduce his heroin use, Parker had frequently turned to liquor. Alcohol, however, did not prove to be a wise alternative, for it aggravated his stomach ulcers and worsened the bleeding. Ironically, heroin provided him with the most effective relief from the agony caused by his bleeding ulcers. For the next several years, he would follow this destructive cycle as he continued to require some regular form of chemical escape from the pressures of his life.

At the end of 1950, however, Parker was in such severe pain that he could not afford to avoid proper treatment any longer. As soon as he returned from Europe, he checked into a hospital. The doctors treated him and then released him, repeating past warnings that without great changes in his life-style, his health would only deteriorate. ❧

11

"BIRD OF PARADISE"

B Y THE START of 1951, Charlie Parker had found happiness in his personal life. For the first time since childhood, he had settled into a conventional routine. Living with Chan Parker and her daughter, Kim, gave the saxophonist the opportunity to experience a stable family environment after 15 years of rootlessness, and he discovered that domestic life was very much to his liking. He loved being a father to Kim and was overjoyed when Chan gave birth to a second daughter, Pree, in 1952 and a son, Baird, the following year. They all moved into a brownstone on New York City's Lower East Side, a lower-middle-class neighborhood that was home to a mixture of ethnic groups.

Unfortunately for Parker, 1951 also saw his history of heroin use lead to major problems. Despite having been addicted to heroin for more than 15 years, he had never been arrested on drug possession charges, even though the police, in New York and elsewhere, were aware of his reputation as a drug user. Dealers and other addicts could often be found backstage or outside the clubs where Parker performed, with narcotics detectives lurking constantly in the shadows, hoping to catch the saxophonist in possession of heroin or some other illegal drug. Somehow, Parker always sensed when the police were about to approach him, and he managed to avoid an arrest and conviction.

Parker enjoys a night on the town with Chan, his common-law wife, who provided him with the only period of domestic happiness he experienced after his childhood. They lived together for most of the saxophonist's last five years.

Awaiting the start of a benefit concert, Parker lingers outside Harlem's Rockland Palace in September 1952 with baritone saxophonist Gerry Mulligan, one of the pioneers of cool jazz. "An odd thing about Bird's influence," said clarinetist Tony Scott, "is that the style he was so influential in developing was played on all instruments but his own horn— the alto. The reason was that Bird was so supreme on the alto."

In 1951, the police took a different tack. Knowing they did not have to hold a hearing or a trial, let alone obtain a conviction, to have Parker's cabaret card taken away, the police asked the New York State Liquor Authority to revoke his permit on the grounds that he had been associating with drug dealers and users. That June, the 30-year-old musician was forced to surrender his card.

The result was a financial disaster. Without a permit, Parker was not allowed to work at nightclubs in New York State. He was still free to perform in the state at concert halls and recording sessions and to seek gigs in nightclubs outside the state. Playing at New York City cabarets, however, had long been his steadiest source of income.

Losing the cabaret card hurt Parker in other ways. To support his family, he was forced to accept engagements that required him to be on the road for weeks or even months at a time, and he hated the constant touring because it kept him apart from his family. He also felt that the audiences on these tours did not fully appreciate modern jazz.

Because the money Parker earned from his out-of-town engagements was significantly less than what he made in New York, he could not afford to keep a band together. Instead, he generally worked as a single, arriving in a city on his own and playing with a group of local musicians. On most occasions, he never even got a chance to rehearse with the other players before the show began. Consequently, their performances usually lacked precision and cohesiveness.

While Parker was drifting ever further away from the New York jazz scene, bebop proceeded to lose a significant portion of its audience to other kinds of music, especially pop music and dance-oriented rhythm and blues. As the number of jazz listeners dwindled, nightclubs grew emptier, fewer jazz records were sold, and the number of jobs that were available to jazz musicians decreased. At the same time, modern jazz headed in a new direction, building on the ideas and developments introduced by Parker and his fellow beboppers.

This movement was nicknamed cool jazz, and among its pioneers were Miles Davis, whose new music stressed harmonic complexity over bebop's rhythmic innovations; tenor saxophonist Stan Getz, who offered a marriage of bebop's concepts with the elegant swing of Lester Young; and baritone saxophonist and composer Gerry Mulligan. Their music sounded reserved and less dramatic than bebop, and it caught on fairly rapidly. By 1953, cool jazz had largely replaced bebop as the most popular style among listeners of modern jazz.

Parker had no strong interest in cool jazz and never explored the new style. His recordings and performances during the early 1950s saw him attempting to match his past achievements in the bebop revolution. Accordingly, he found himself being left behind as jazz continued to evolve.

Parker still proved capable of producing great music, such as when he played at the September 1952 benefit dance at Harlem's Rockland Palace. Performing with a quintet and with Bird with Strings, he displayed much of his classic inspiration and fire. Yet by 1953, his style of jazz ceased to matter to most critics and listeners. In the span of just a few years, they had come to regard Parker's music as routine and dated.

In March 1953, for example, Parker traveled to Canada for a bebop reunion concert at Massey Hall in Toronto. The auditorium was less than half full, even though he was slated to appear with Dizzy Gillespie, Bud Powell, and Max Roach—three of the four musicians who had shared the stage with him at the Three Deuces eight years earlier. Rounding out

A 1953 bebop celebration at Toronto's Massey Hall reunited Parker (far right) with Dizzy Gillespie (second from right), Max Roach (center), and Bud Powell (far left). Rounding out the quintet was bassist Charles Mingus, who brought a tape recorder onstage and captured the remarkable concert, perhaps the finest in bebop history.

the quintet was bassist Charles Mingus, a late replacement for Oscar Pettiford.

Parker and the other musicians played brilliantly at Massey Hall, performing with as much fire and energy as ever the tunes that had changed the direction of jazz. For one night, all the problems of the past few years seemed to disappear. The concert marked one of bebop's finest hours, as well as the last time Parker, Gillespie, Powell, and Roach ever shared a stage. (Much to the good fortune of jazz fans everywhere, Mingus brought a tape recorder onstage and captured this celebrated concert. It has since been released on record as *The Greatest Jazz Concert Ever* and on compact disc as *The Quintet: Jazz at Massey Hall.*)

Such great performances became increasingly rare for Parker. The exhausting routine of playing night after night, often far from home, before indifferent audiences, seemed to wear him down. His once dynamic, playful spirit disappeared behind a mask of fatigue and indifference. Performing was no longer fulfilling; it had turned into a burden from which he knew no escape.

Parker's declining physical health did not help matters. His stomach ulcers and heart trouble had continued to worsen, and he did little to halt their deterioration. Moreover, he had begun to suffer serious bouts of depression.

Not even the restoration of Parker's cabaret card in August 1953 could lift his spirits very much. Having earned a reputation for being troublesome and undependable, he received few offers to play in New York City nightclubs. To help make ends meet, he appeared in a series of Sunday afternoon concerts in Greenwich Village and continued to perform at out-of-town engagements. Sometimes he toured with the Stan Kenton Orchestra or another band as a guest soloist. Yet he continued to be so strapped for money that he accepted almost any gig he was offered.

In the wake of such financial difficulties, tragedy arrived. Parker and Chan could not afford the expert care of a private hospital when two-year-old Pree became ill with a heart condition; instead, they brought their daughter to public clinics and hospitals for treatment. Parker was on tour in early 1954 when Chan phoned him with the heartrending news that the child had died. Maintaining that Pree's death was his fault because he had been unable to provide her with better medical care, he allowed himself to be plagued by tremendous guilt, convinced that his career failures had cost his daughter her life.

Parker's gloomy mood finally erupted in a fit of anger during a performance at Birdland in the

The jazz revolutionary, near the end of his troubled life.

late summer of 1954. Appearing at his familiar haunt with Bird with Strings, he quarreled with the other musicians and fired the string section in mid-performance. Birdland's management turned right around and barred Parker from playing at the club that had been named in his honor.

Parker returned home from that awful evening only to enter a heated argument with his wife. Still feeling angry, depressed, and confused after their exchange, he went into the bathroom, took a bottle of iodine from the medicine cabinet, and drank the poison, intent on dying. Chan helped save her husband's life by rushing him to Bellevue Hospital, where he had his stomach pumped.

Parker spent the next week and a half in the hospital's mental ward. By the end of that 10-day stretch, his doctors were satisfied that he was no longer seriously disturbed and released him. Several weeks later, however, he again began to feel severely depressed and suicidal, and he voluntarily reentered the hospital for another two weeks of psychiatric treatment. This time upon his release, he left New York with Chan and the children and went to rural Pennsylvania, where he continued his recuperation in a house owned by his wife's family.

When Parker returned to New York that fall, he performed infrequently. For the most part, his professional appearances were limited to second-rate clubs and informal sessions in Greenwich Village. But even with his physical and mental health failing, he was still capable of approaching his past greatness. In October, he performed at Town Hall, where he played well before a small audience.

There were not enough triumphs, however, to carry Parker through this dark period. He separated from Chan and returned to his wandering ways, relying on his few remaining friends for a place to sleep or a decent meal. Whenever he was unable to spend the night in someone's home, he would ride the subways or bed down on a street in Greenwich Village.

Homeless, overwhelmed by depression, and in constant pain from his ulcers and heart condition, Parker did not seem to care what was happening to him. At any rate, he was powerless to stop his world from crumbling. By now, he no longer depended on heroin and hard liquor to tide him through his black moods. Instead, he gulped heart pills and painkillers prescribed by his doctors and washed the medication down with cheap wine.

Friends who were concerned for Parker's well-being helped arrange his return to Birdland in early March 1955. It was a final chance to restart a career that had all but ended. Sadly, the saxophonist let the opportunity for a big comeback slip away on the night of March 5.

Four days later, Parker set out for an engagement in Boston. He started to feel extremely ill after only a few minutes of traveling, so he stopped to recuperate at the Fifth Avenue apartment of Baroness Pannonica de Koenigswarter. Over the years, Nica, as the baroness was known to her friends, had come to the aid of many jazz musicians. "She saw to it," recalled Gillespie, "that a lot of guys who had no place to stay had a roof or put some money in their pockets."

An ailing Parker was a familiar sight at the baroness's apartment. This time, however, she saw he was in greater pain than usual and summoned a doctor. Parker's condition greatly alarmed the physician, who insisted that the musician be hospitalized immediately. Parker stubbornly refused, believing, as always, that he would recover if he got a little rest.

With the baroness and her daughter keeping a close eye on him, Parker remained at the apartment for three days. By Saturday, March 12, the sharp pain had subsided, and he felt well enough to relax in front of a television set. He was laughing heartily at a juggling act on the screen when, all of a sudden, he began to choke and gasp for breath. In a few minutes, he was dead.

The doctor who examined Parker's body pronounced the cause of death as a heart attack, listing pneumonia, ulcers, and cirrhosis of the liver as contributing factors. Based on these ailments and the deteriorated physical condition of the deceased, the doctor estimated Parker's age as 53. He was in fact just five and a half months shy of his 35th birthday.

As Parker passed into jazz history, his reputation grew rapidly, as if his enormous contributions to jazz could be truly appreciated only after his death. Within a matter of months, the slogan *Bird Lives* began to appear on walls and sidewalks all over New York City. The saxophonist's life may have ended, but his spirit had survived.

And so did his music. Parker's influence on modern jazz has since proven to be so far-reaching that almost every development in the four decades since his death can be traced to the exceptional originality and complexity of his music. Today, his best recordings remain available; his compositions are performed frequently; and his sound and playing style on the alto saxophone are often imitated, although they are never matched. As much as ever, Charlie Parker's music remains the living embodiment of his incomparable, irreplaceable genius. ⬥

APPENDIX:
SELECTED DISCOGRAPHY

The only way to truly appreciate Charlie Parker's tremendous musical genius is to listen to his recordings. There are many records, cassettes, and compact discs to choose from, however, because most of his studio and live recordings have been released numerous times since his death.

The Dial and Savoy labels offer the best introduction to Parker's studio sessions, for their cuts feature the saxophonist at the peak of his creative powers. The Dial sessions have been released several times by a number of different companies. The best available package at present is *Charlie Parker: The Legendary Dial Masters, Volumes 1 and 2* on the Stash label; both volumes are on compact disc only. The Savoy sessions still appear under the original company's name and are available in all recording formats. The best package of the Savoy material is *Bird/Savoy Original Master Takes*, a two-compact-disc set.

Parker's earliest studio recordings with the Jay McShann Orchestra are currently unavailable. But his wonderful 1945 Guild recordings with Dizzy Gillespie have been released by Musicraft as part of *Shaw 'Nuff*. This album, credited to Dizzy Gillespie & His Sextets and Orchestra, also features some of the trumpeter's outstanding recordings without Parker.

Parker's later recordings, for the Mercury label, are now available on Verve Records. Many of these recordings feature him with backing musicians or orchestras that greatly detract from the quality of his music. Several of these compilations on compact disc are worth hearing and owning, however, such as *The Original Recordings of Charlie Parker* and *Compact Jazz*.

There are many live recordings of Parker's music available on a wide variety of record labels. While the music on these releases can be quite wonderful, the recording quality is often quite poor because many of the performances were radio broadcasts recorded on very primitive equipment. These releases usually offer little or no information regarding the source of the recordings, and they should probably be avoided by all but the most enthusiastic listeners. Among the best of these recordings is *Bird at the Roost, Volumes 1 through 4*, which consists of radio broadcasts from the Royal Roost nightclub in late 1948 and early 1949.

Jazz at Massey Hall, on the Original Jazz Classics (OJC) label, is one live performance that certainly makes for worthwhile listening. Credited to the Quintet of the Year, this 1953 concert in Toronto, Canada, which reunited Parker with Dizzy Gillespie, Bud Powell, and Max Roach, also serves as a perfect introduction to the excitement of bebop.

CHRONOLOGY

———— ❦ ————

1920   Born Charles Parker, Jr., on August 29 in Kansas City, Kansas

1928   Moves to Kansas City, Missouri

1933   Enrolls in Lincoln High School music course and learns to play his first musical instrument, a baritone horn

1934   Joins his first band, the Deans of Swing, as a saxophonist

1936   Humiliates himself at a Reno Club jam session; marries first wife, Rebecca Ruffin; begins to perform with regional bands

1937   Becomes a protégé of Buster Smith's

1938   First son, Francis Leon, is born; Parker discovers a new approach to jazz improvisation while jamming in New York City

1939   Joins the Jay McShann Orchestra

1940   Makes his first recordings

1942   Settles in New York City; joins the Earl Hines Orchestra

1943   Marries second wife, Geraldine Scott; makes first recordings with Dizzy Gillespie

1944   Joins the Billy Eckstine Orchestra; performs with Gillespie at the Three Deuces

1945   Leads his own ensemble for the first time; makes his West Coast debut

1946   Makes first recordings for Dial Records; suffers a nervous breakdown and is committed to Camarillo State Hospital

1947   Released from Camarillo; forms quintet that includes Miles Davis; records extensively for the Dial and Savoy record labels; performs at Carnegie Hall as featured guest of the Dizzy Gillespie Orchestra; tours with his quintet as part of Jazz at the Philharmonic

1948   Signs with Mercury Records; marries third wife, Doris Sydnor

1949   Performs at the second annual Paris Jazz Festival; takes part in the first Bird with Strings recording session; resumes relationship with Chan Richardson; headlines at the opening of Birdland; performs with his quintet at the Modern Jazz All-Star Concert at Carnegie Hall

1950   Makes second tour of Europe

1951   Loses his cabaret card and is unable to accept engagements at New York City nightclubs

1952   Daughter, Pree, is born

1953   Second son, Baird, is born; Parker performs at Massey Hall reunion concert in Toronto

1954   Pree dies; Parker is barred from playing at Birdland; has difficulty in finding engagements; attempts suicide; separates from Chan

1955   Dies of a heart attack, with pneumonia, ulcers, and cirrhosis of the liver as contributing factors, on March 12 in New York City

FURTHER READING

Chambers, Jack. *Milestones One: The Music and Times of Miles Davis to 1960*. New York: Morrow, 1983.

———. *Milestones Two: The Music and Times of Miles Davis Since 1960*. New York: Morrow, 1985.

Collier, James Lincoln. *The Making of Jazz: A Comprehensive History*. New York: Dell, 1979.

Crow, Bill. *Jazz Anecdotes*. New York: Oxford University Press, 1990.

Davis, Miles, with Quincy Troupe. *Miles: The Autobiography*. New York: Simon & Schuster, 1989.

Frankl, Ron. *Duke Ellington*. New York: Chelsea House, 1988.

Gentry, Tony. *Dizzy Gillespie*. New York: Chelsea House, 1991.

Giddins, Gary. *Celebrating Bird: The Triumph of Charlie Parker*. New York: Morrow, 1987.

Gillespie, Dizzy, with Al Fraser. *To Be or Not to Bop*. New York: Doubleday, 1979.

Gitler, Ira. *Swing to Bop*. New York: Oxford University Press, 1985.

Lyons, Len, and Don Perlo. *Jazz Portraits*. New York: Morrow, 1989.

Priestley, Brian. *Charlie Parker*. New York: Hippocrene Books, 1984.

Reisner, Robert, ed. *Bird: The Legend of Charlie Parker*. New York: Citadel Press, 1962.

Russell, Ross. *Bird Lives!* London: Quartet Books, 1973.

———. *Jazz Style in Kansas City and the Southwest*. Berkeley: University of California Press, 1982.

Tanenhaus, Sam. *Louis Armstrong*. New York: Chelsea House, 1989.

INDEX

American Federation of
Musicians (AFM), 59, 60, 95
Armstrong, Louis, 24, 61, 75

bebop, 11–12, 52, 56, 57, 59, 60,
62–65, 68–70, 73–75, 79, 80,
82–85, 91, 93, 99, 107, 108,
112–13
Basie, William ("Count"), 43,
44, 47, 55
Bechet, Sidney, 102
Belafonte, Harry, 13
Berg, Billy, 81–84
"Billy's Bounce," 80
Birdland, 11, 13–19, 105, 106,
115–18
"Bird of Paradise," 94, 106
Bird with Strings, 104–7, 113,
117
Blakey, Art, 15, 17, 18
"Bloomdido," 107
Blue Devils, 44
Brown, Ray, 70, 82
Brown, Walter, 54, 56

Camarillo State Hospital, 87,
89–90
Carter, Benny, 44, 53, 84
"Cheers," 90
"Cherokee," 50–52, 54, 72, 79,
82
Chicago, Illinois, 48, 49, 56,
95
Clarke, Kenny, 57
Clayton, Buck, 44
Columbia Records, 59, 60
"Cool Blues," 90
Cool jazz, 113
Count Basie Orchestra, 34, 43,
44, 60, 102

Dallas, Texas, 56
Dameron, Tadd, 52, 75
Daniels, Ernest, 39
Davis, Miles, 12, 79, 84, 91, 96,
100, 102, 113
Deans of Swing, 27, 30, 31, 35,
55
Decca Records, 56, 59, 60
"Dexterity," 94
Dial Records, 85, 86, 90, 91,
93–94
Dorham, McKinley ("Kenny"),
15, 17, 18, 100, 104
Douglas, Tommy, 41, 44
Du Bois, W. E. B., 42
Duke Ellington Orchestra, 44,
68

Eckstine, Billy, 48, 62, 63, 64,
65, 68
Eldridge, Roy, 71
Ellington, Duke, 24
"Embraceable You," 94
Evans, Herschel, 31, 44

52nd Street ("the Street"), 67–
69, 75, 77, 81, 84, 92
Finale Club, 84, 86
Fleet, Buddy, 50
Fuller, Gil, 75

Gardner, Goon, 48, 49
Garrett, Duke, 74
Gershwin, George, 69
Gershwin, Ira, 69
Getz, Stan, 13, 113
Gillespie, John ("Dizzy"), 12,
13, 57, 60, 62–63, 64, 65,
67, 70–75, 79, 80–82, 91,
94–95, 107–8, 113–14, 118
Gillespie, Lorraine Willis, 72

Goodstein, Oscar, 17
Guild Records, 74

Haig, Al, 82, 100, 106
Harris, Little Benny, 62
Hawkins, Coleman, 67, 68, 74
Haynes, Roy, 104
Hines, Earl, 61, 62, 63, 64
Hodges, Johnny, 44, 53
Holiday, Billie, 44
"Hymn, The," 94

"I Got Rhythm," 72

Jackson, Milt, 81, 82
Jacquet, Illinois, 74
Jazz at the Philharmonic, 83,
95, 104, 107
Jimmy's Chicken Shack, 49
Johnson, Budd, 31, 62
Jones, Jo, 34, 36
Jordan, Duke, 91, 104

Kansas City, Kansas, 23, 24
Kansas City, Missouri, 21–24,
26, 31, 34, 36, 37, 39, 44,
47, 52, 64
Kansas City Rockets, 44, 52
Kansas City–style jazz, 21–22,
44
Kenton, Stan, 115
Keyes, Lawrence, 31, 32, 36, 42
Kirk, Andy, 44, 47, 55, 60, 64
Koenigswarter, Baroness Pan-
nonica de, 118
"Ko Ko," 79–80

"Leap Frog," 107
Lee, George E., 42
Leonard, Harlan, 44, 52

Lincoln High School, 26, 27, 31, 32
Los Angeles, California, 81–86, 91
"Lover Man," 86–87, 91

McGhee, Howard, 84, 86, 91
McShann, Jay, 47, 52–57
Massey Hall concert, 113–14
Mercury Records, 95, 100–102, 104
Mingus, Charles, 15, 17, 18
Minton's Playhouse, 57, 60, 68
Monk, Thelonious, 12, 57, 60, 73, 107
Monroe's Uptown House, 50, 57, 60
"Moose the Mooche," 86
Morton, Benny, 44
Mulligan, Gerry, 113
Music theory, 29–30, 36–37, 50, 73, 79, 103
"My Old Flame," 94

Navarro, Fats, 107
"Now's the Time," 80

"Ornithology," 86
"Out of Nowhere," 94
Ozark Mountains, 39, 41

Page, Oran ("Hot Lips"), 67, 102
Paris Jazz Festival, 102
Parker, Addie (mother), 23, 24, 26, 48, 53
Parker, Baird (son), 111
Parker, Chan (fourth wife), 14, 77, 105, 111, 115, 117
Parker, Charles, Sr. (father), 23, 24, 52
Parker, Charlie
  begins to play the saxophone, 26

and the Billy Eckstine Orchestra, 64–65, 68
birth and childhood, 23–27
collaboration with Dizzy Gillespie, 70–75, 79, 81–84, 94–95, 107–8, 113–14
"comeback" at Birdland, 11, 14–19
common-law marriage to Chan Parker, 14, 105, 111, 115, 117
death, 119
drug and alcohol addiction, 14, 15, 18, 41–42, 48, 52, 60–61, 63–64, 71, 72, 83–84, 86, 90, 92, 96–97, 108–9, 111, 118
discovers new improvisational technique, 50–51
and the Earl Hines Orchestra, 61–64
first recording, 55
health problems, 15, 39, 108–9, 115, 118–19
homeless, 117–18
humiliated at the Reno Club, 34–36
irresponsible with money, 78–79, 93
and the Jay McShann Orchestra, 52–57, 59, 60, 61
joins his first band, 27
loses his cabaret card, 14, 112, 115
marriage, 14, 33, 47–48, 53, 63, 77, 96, 105, 111, 115, 117
musical education, 29–37, 41, 42–43, 44–45, 50, 103
nicknamed Yardbird, 11, 53–54, 79
saxophones, 26, 40, 62, 90
suicide attempt, 117
Parker, Doris (third wife), 77, 90, 96, 105

Parker, Francis Leon (son), 47, 53
Parker, Geraldine (second wife), 63
Parker, John (half-brother), 23
Parker, Kim (daughter), 111
Parker, Pree (daughter), 111, 115
Parker, Rebecca (first wife), 32, 33, 47–48, 53
Pettiford, Oscar, 114
Powell, Bud, 12, 15–19, 70, 106, 113–14

Ramey, Gene, 27, 36, 55
Randolph, A. Philip, 42
Redcross, Bob, 63, 65, 69
"Red Cross," 69, 70
"Relaxin' at Camarillo," 90
Reno Club, 33–36
Rich, Buddy, 108
Richardson, Chan. See Parker, Chan
Roach, Max, 70, 79, 91, 92, 104, 113–14
Rodney, Red, 104, 106, 107
Royal Roost, 12, 95, 96, 100
Ruffin, Fanny, 32, 33
Ruffin, Rebecca. See Parker, Rebecca
Rushing, Jimmy, 44
Russell, Curley, 79
Russell, Ross, 85–87, 90, 94

Savoy Records, 69, 80, 93–95
Scott, Geraldine. See Parker, Geraldine
"Scrapple from the Apple," 94
Shaw, Billy, 81
Simpson, Robert, 32
Sissle, Noble, 63
65 Club, 48
Smith, Bessie, 24
Smith, Buster ("Prof"), 44–45, 47, 49, 52

Swing, 11, 43–44, 53, 57, 59, 60, 62, 68, 69, 70, 71, 73, 83
Sydnor, Doris. *See* Parker, Doris

Tatum, Art, 49, 50
Three Deuces, 70, 71, 73, 74, 91, 113

"Tiny's Tempo," 69, 70
To Be or Not To Bop (Gillespie), 71
Town Hall, 74, 114
Tristano, Lennie, 16

Vaughan, Sarah, 62, 63, 64
Victor Records, 59, 60

Webster, Ben, 31, 67, 68, 69
Wells, Dickie, 44
White, Walter, 42
Wilkerson, George, 39

"Yardbird Suite," 86
Young, Lester, 13, 31, 35, 37, 43, 44, 55, 83, 113

PICTURE CREDITS

RON FRANKL was born in New York City and is a graduate of Haverford College. He is a longtime Charlie Parker fan and owns more than 1,500 jazz recordings, including more than 100 hours of the saxophonist's recorded music. Mr. Frankl is also the author of *Duke Ellington* in Chelsea House's BLACK AMERICANS OF ACHIEVEMENT series.

NATHAN IRVIN HUGGINS, one of America's leading scholars in the field of black studies, helped select the titles for the BLACK AMERICANS OF ACHIEVEMENT series, for which he also served as senior consulting editor. He was the W.E.B. Du Bois Professor of History and of Afro-American Studies at Harvard University and the director of the W.E.B. Du Bois Institute for Afro-American Research at Harvard. He received his doctorate from Harvard in 1962 and returned there as a professor in 1980 after teaching at Columbia University, the University of Massachusetts, Lake Forest College, and the California State University, Long Beach. He was the author of four books and dozens of articles, including *Black Odyssey: The Afro-American Ordeal in Slavery*, *The Harlem Renaissance*, and *Slave and Citizen: The Life of Frederick Douglass*, and was associated with the Children's Television Workshop, National Public Radio, the Boston Athenaeum, the Museum of Afro-American History, the Howard Thurman Educational Trust, and Upward Bound. Professor Huggins died in 1989, at the age of 62, in Cambridge, Massachusetts.